The Hallelujah Life

Richard D. Propes

Heart n' Sole Press

THE HALLELUJAH LIFE
Copyright © 2012 Heart n' Sole Press

All rights reserved. Printed in the United States. No part of this book may be used or reproduced, stored in a retrieval system, or transmitted, in any form or by any means, electronic, mechanical, photocopying, recording or otherwise, without written permission from the publisher except in the case of brief quotations embodied in critical articles and reviews. For information, contact Heart n' Sole Press, 5115 Devon Drive, Indianapolis, IN 46226 or visit the book's website at www.thehallelujahlife.com

ISBN: 061562202X
ISBN-13: 978-0615622026

DEDICATION

The Hallelujah Life is dedicated to all those who have inspired me to live a life of ordinary greatness. This includes God, my daughter Jennifer, my goddaughter Victoria, the nurses at Wishard Memorial Hospital, Mrs. Pruitt in first grade, Valerie, Victor, Laura, "Ma" Booth, Lisa, Christina, Melissa M., Melissa G., Celeste, Jeff, Phil, Louie, Robyn, Anne, Jack and Grace Propes, Joshua Propes, my nephews, Bob W., Michelle, Harriet, everyone who has ever volunteered for the Tenderness Tour, Sister Marian Ruth, Father Boniface, Amy B., John Callahan, Laura D., John Hiatt, Peace Pilgrim and many others whose many gifts to my life will never be forgotten.

ACKNOWLEDGMENTS

I am most grateful to those who have been relentless in their commitment to my emotional and physical well-being. In the darkest moments of my life, there has always been at least one person who refused to let go and who stood by me when so many others simply gave up. To those of you who have never let go, I say "Thank you!"

A Brief Observation

This is not the life
 I had planned.

Richard Propes

I Had a Dream

I wanted to look in the mirror
and feel like I was enough.

I wanted to lie naked with you
and not see the scars and the lines and the memories.

I wanted to remember myself
as beloved.

I wanted to live within my body
comfortably and joyfully.

I wanted to have sex
standing up.

I wanted to hold you
without fearing that I'm hurting you.

I wanted to be in a crowded room
and not feel so alone.

I wanted you to know I'd give you anything
even though I had nothing.

I had a dream.

Certain Truths

There are certain truths
on which I will not compromise.

Violence is
never justified.

Love is
more powerful than hate.

Kissing is
sublime.

Peace is
always possible.

Forgiveness is
absolutely required.

Breaking the cycle is
not a lonely endeavor.

God is
not made in our image.

Humor is
the best medicine.

Sex is
a close second.

Sushi is
disgusting.

Chaplin's "City Lights" is
the best movie ever made.

The best place for gimp sex in Indianapolis is
Crown Hill Cemetery.

Lucas Oil Stadium is
a close second.

Touch is
essential.

Laundry is
more difficult than it looks.

Loving others is
 the key to happiness.

A tattoo of your true love's name is
a bad idea.

Equality is
what Jesus would do.

Prayer is
the most intimate act two people can share.

The Bible is
best placed in the humor section of a bookstore.

Shame is
a waste of valuable time.

Anger is
a close second.

Every moment in life is
an opportunity to love someone.

THE HALLELUJAH LIFE

The God I Believe In

Most people find it ludicrous when I say
that I felt God's presence that day on the playground.

"If God was really with you," they exclaim,
"Why didn't he reach down and pluck you right out
of that sandbox and out of harm's way?"

I just chuckle.

I've never believed in a plucking God,
but in a God who would walk with me through the fire.

I believe in a God who would be raped right alongside me,
feeling my pain
and
experiencing my humiliation.

I believe in a God
whose love is more powerful than hate
and who dwells within
every scar
and every memory.

I believe in a God
who never lets go
and who fights like hell
so that I will never forget what it means to be loved.

Richard Propes

My First Memory

I was five-years-old and naked with a girl I didn't know.

The old man just sat there beside the bed,
giggling as he placed her naked body
on top of mine.

He would fondle himself with one hand,
while taking photographs
long since destroyed
but never forgotten.

I still get embarrassed even thinking about it,
and I can't help but wonder whatever happened
to old what's 'er name.

What was her name?

I wish I could remember.

I wonder if she realizes
that she has a leading role in my first memory.

Why can't I remember anything before this day?

I want to remember.
I need to remember.

If I can't remember innocence,
then how can it possibly be true?

THE HALLELUJAH LIFE

Barney Fife

I met Barney Fife on the day I was born,
or at least this is what I've been told by the Lebanon Daily Reporter,
the newspaper for a town small enough where such a meeting was
considered to be worthy of front page coverage.

From what I've read,
Barney just sort of happened upon my parents
on the highway just outside of town
a flat tire having delayed
the inevitable birth of their soon to be demon child.

That would be me.

I can't help but wonder if he said
"Nip it in the bud" or if just maybe
he had a bullet in his pocket.

All I know for certain is that somehow
Barney Fife came through that day
as Barney Fife always did.

October 1, 1965.

It was the day I was born
and I reckon I was innocent
at least for a few hours or so.

Mrs. Stubbs

I spent the first few weeks of my life in a full-body cast,
depending upon the kindness of strangers
in a world I'd imagine didn't make much sense and still doesn't.

Hugging doesn't come naturally for me, perhaps a remnant of those days hooked up to tubes
and wires
and monitors
without a semblance of humanity other than these strange little ladies
in white hats
with smiling faces.

I don't remember these days at all, but I have the sneaking suspicion I survived them.

I didn't recognize Mrs. Stubbs standing outside the drug store parking lot, but she had that look in her eyes and I knew that she knew that I knew that she knew.

Something.

I figured she was just another Jehovah's Witness determined to tell me the truth that would lead to my eternal life.

She wasn't but she did.

Mrs. Stubbs remembers my innocence.

She was there the day I was born, all 6-lbs and 8 oz. of me fighting to survive Barney Fife and spina bifida and a world that didn't quite know how to keep me alive but was fighting like hell to do so.

"We always remembered the babies like you who stayed with us for a long time," Mrs. Stubbs explained very matter-of-factly. "I've never forgotten your smile," she claimed

as I climbed back into my car
my head turned away
and tears streaming down my face.

"She remembered my smile," I said to myself,
an inescapable truth confirming
finally
irrevocably
that I was born a happy child.

Richard Propes

A Reflection on Birth

There is very little I regret about having "come out" as a survivor of sexual abuse. There is very little I regret about having told truths about my past, my childhood, my family and my mistakes along the way. What I do regret, and I regret it deeply, is the degree to which I was unprepared for the ways in which my healing journey has hurt my parents.

I was born on October 1, 1965 with spina bifida. One of the most common congenital birth defects, in 1965 spina bifida led to the death or severe disabling of nearly 95% of those infants born with it. An overwhelming majority of babies that did survive being born with spina bifida during this time period would either end up dying young, living with severe developmental disabilities and/or were expected to be physically dependent for their entire lives. Given that I had been further challenged by a delay in getting to the hospital and was born in a smaller, ill-equipped hospital, virtually no one expected my survival.

One of my favorite stories from my mother is how after I was born, doctors were preparing her for the worst possible outcome. My mother's priest suggested to her that perhaps it would be best if I did not survive. "Perhaps, it is God's will," she tells me he said.

When I finally asked my mother about her response to all of these events occurring in the life of a 20-year-old newlywed, she stated very simply "I gave your life to God." The weirdest thing for me is that as she made this statement, "I gave your life to God," the glow on her face revealed that she truly believed that she was giving a "gift" to God. I learned a lot about my mother during this conversation, and even if everything else she ever did as a parent was a failure it would be these actions in my earliest days that would later help define my relentless commitment to life and ability. I will be eternally grateful for her absolute refusal to give up and her complete faith that this seriously disabled child was a "gift" for her for however long she was blessed to have me in her life.

My parents could have easily given up on this little baby that nobody expected to survive and, even if I did survive, everyone expected to have severe physical and developmental challenges that would be life-long.

My parents lived the better part of eighteen years barely surviving financially because virtually their entire existence centered around my 50+ surgeries and doing whatever they could do to ensure my surviving and thriving with as normal a childhood as possible. My parents, without question, compromised their own dreams to raise me. While in many ways they were ill-equipped for parenting, they were steadfast in their commitment to my welfare through it all.

My childhood wasn't a fairy tale and in many ways my relationship with my parents became increasingly strained as I moved into young adulthood. My parents weren't and aren't perfect, but their refusal to ever give up on me has turned me into a human being who relentlessly refuses to give up on myself and others.

One of my greatest sorrows has been the poor way I handled my initial "coming out" as a survivor of sexual abuse. While there were many challenging experiences within the family home growing up, I was not prepared for the onslaught of media attention and skewed interpretation of my written and spoken words that ended up casting my parents in a far more negative light than they deserved. It taught me one of my earliest and most valued lessons - that being a survivor of abuse does not give one a green light to abuse others. We must always be on guard that our words are an accurate reflection of our experiences and that our actions do not perpetuate the cycles we are trying to end.

My parents have fought like hell for me virtually every day of their lives. While I still speak my truth and acknowledge the challenges I faced growing up, I also hope that my life is a reflection of my gratitude for all the ways in which they loved me fully into life.

Richard Propes

A Reflection On My Family

I grew up in a confusing home. I am a survivor because my parents refused to ever accept less. My parents always believed in my ability to transcend my circumstances, though they weren't always good at communicating that belief. My parents lived on very little while I was growing up, mostly because they were so absolutely committed to giving me the best opportunities for success they could. Both of my parents were more practical in nature. It was important to them to provide a good home, make sure my basic needs were cared for and make sure my medical needs were met.

I was closest to my mother, both a result of our mutual involvement in church activities with Jehovah's Witnesses and my father's complete inability to deal with my disability early in life. I remember summer after summer of attending district conferences throughout the Midwest. I also remember my mother's constant attendance at the hospital during my many surgeries, and her enthusiastic support of virtually any activity I requested ranging from Putt-Putt leagues to Speech Team to my managing of a variety of school sports teams.

My mother longed for me to have as normal a life as possible, but my personal needs, difficulties with self-care and the more intimate aspects of spina bifida made it difficult to form friendships, go to parties, attend sleepovers or do many of the things that healthier children and youth do as part of growing up.

Wherever I stayed, someone had to be comfortable assisting me with very intimate needs such as attending my ostomy and helping with bathroom requirements. My mother had one sister who did quite well with it, while my father had a couple sisters who thought nothing of assisting me and openly and warmly welcomed me into their homes.

My mother grew up as one of five siblings in a working middle-class family that was devoutly Catholic. She was fairly liberal, which made her a bit of a black sheep in her otherwise conservative family. I would imagine her parents cringed a bit when she met the man who would become her husband and my father, a bit of a bad boy from Kentucky who left home in his mid teenage years and was likely more working class than they'd have liked.

I've often described my mother as a greeting card, a perpetual optimist even when her entire life is falling apart around her. My relationship with my mother changed dramatically both when news of my sexual abuse surfaced and as our time with Jehovah's Witnesses came to a close. My mother had worked very hard my entire life to protect me, and I think the idea that abuse occurred anyway has felt like a failure to her.

The truth is that she didn't fail, though in that same breath I'd have no trouble acknowledging that my home life was far from perfect. Being a Jehovah's Witness, while filled with much joy for many years, also added a layer of stress at school and between my parents.

My parents were still children when I was born, at least on some level. They married at ages 19 and 20, respectively, and I was born a little over nine months later. They were ill-equipped to handle a disabled child when I was born. I've always believed that if they'd have had a chance to be married for several years prior to my birth, they'd have either been much different parents or they'd have divorced. I don't believe the disability was entirely the problem, and I certainly don't blame myself for their early married life conflicts. Personally, I think that having any child as soon as they did would have been challenging for them. However, having a child with a disability really compounded the stress for my parents.

My father was born in the hills of Kentucky. He was one of 10 siblings growing up in a small house with no plumbing, an outhouse and an alcoholic, abusive father. By the time I was old enough to really remember our Kentucky visits, however, my grandfather was sober and had calmed down considerably. I loved visiting all of my Kentucky relatives, and one of my greater regrets in life may be never having moved to Kentucky.

My father grew up with quite a few challenges, most of which I won't share because they're his business. It's safe to say that family cycles did exist within my father's home and these cycles continued within our home as I was growing up.

There came a time, however, when I learned some valuable lessons from my father. There was this point where my mother had reached a breaking point with the conflicts and with his drinking. My father, I'll say honestly to my surprise, gave up drinking and has never looked back, never relapsed and seemingly never regretted the choice. He's become a pretty amazing human being who continues to grow even while wrestling with his own humanity. I was in my thirties when my father first said, at least that I can remember "I love you," and it's only been in recent years that he's grasped hugging. It's been an awesome transformation to watch.

If I'm being honest, I didn't much respect him growing up because he didn't give me much to respect. For the most part, I think he just didn't know how to cope with all he had to face in life. While he certainly visited me when I was hospitalized, it was an experience that clearly made him uncomfortable. I don't excuse the negative behaviors, but as I've grown older I've found it more important to move towards understanding.

I was 12-years-old when my brother was born. Despite our age difference, we grew up very close. He's still famous among my classmates for letting out a big cheer when I won my junior high school spelling bee. If I had any existing doubt about the dysfunctional nature of my home life, however, that doubt was removed when my brother was born.

While I grew up in a culturally diverse inner-city apartment complex, by the time my brother was in junior high my parents had moved up in the world and owned a house on a lake just west of Indianapolis. I've never had any trouble commenting that it was once their disabled child moved out that my parents were finally able to afford to live a better life.

I was one expensive child.

A year or two into my healing journey from sexual abuse, I felt the impulse to call my mother from a local department store. I posed a rather large question "Are you sorry I was born?" I think the question hurt her feelings, but I needed to know the answer or maybe I just needed to hear the answer. I'd always wondered and, quite honestly, I'd have understood a "Yes" answer. Their lives changed dramatically after I was born, and I'm not sure I'd have been able to handle a similar situation myself.

Richard Propes

The First Time

Your mother promised that everything
would be alright.

My mother worried. Incessantly.

I begged. Incessantly.

After a childhood of existing on the outer fringes
of social acceptance,
I was in middle school and about to have my very first sleepover.

Ostomy supplies. Check.
Medications. Check.
Extra clothes. Just in case. Check. Blush.

It seemed that your mother wanted us to get ready for bed
by bathing
together.

I woke up in the middle of the night
with your hand down my pants
fondling
jiggling
giggling.

"I like your penis," you whispered.

Blush.

Before I knew it,
you'd swallowed all of me.

It wasn't exactly an accomplishment,
but still pretty exciting.

THE HALLELUJAH LIFE

The Playground

It has been over twenty years since I felt your body pressed against
mine, your breath invading my thought processes
and your bruised and calloused hands
parting my thighs like Moses parting the Red Sea.

I was bleeding,
but you didn't care.

You laughed. I think.

I'd swear I remember the laughter
as you threw me into the sandbox
and stripped me of my clothing
and my dignity
grabbing what you called my little manhood
and started screaming in my ear
"This is the best you're ever going to get - Say thank you, bitch"
again and again
and again
each thrust met by your piercing scream.

"This is the best you're ever going to get"
is all I can think about
every time another one walks out the door
and I'm left wondering if maybe you were right
or I'm just very, very wrong.

Richard Propes

The Closet

The first time I remember hearing the words "I love you,"
you had me tied up in the closet
as a punishment for my ostomy bag leaking
all over your brand new sheets.

I remember wondering if this was what love
truly felt like
and being absolutely certain
that if so it was something I could live without.

It was in the closet that you put a gun to your brother's head
and said "Suck him!"
So, he did and you laughed before slamming the door shut
and leaving me tied up alone for hours at a time.

You hated it when you heard me praying through the darkness, but
you could never stop it even when you'd flick the lighter
in my crotch time and time again
leaving little burn marks in the shape of a cross.

The Woods

I returned to the woods a few years back
in an effort to convince myself that these disturbing memories
were the truth
or a lie
or something in between.

The tree where you etched your commitment to me was still there,
our initials marking the spot
where you would recreate your sick birthing ritual
over and over again
using stray animals
you would kill for fun
as mommy
or daddy
or some other role that would make you laugh.

I have never understood what happened in the woods
and sometimes I try really hard to convince myself
these memories are too incredible to be true
and I pray to God
that I have remembered everything there is to remember
and I'm not going to have to figure out
how to deal with any new memories.

Richard Propes

Why I've Always Preferred The Black Community

How do you say "Thank you!" to someone who didn't rape you?

It's the little things that mean the most,
like the fact that Tyrone saw you attacking me
and did what no one had ever done before.

He kicked your ass.

Royally.

I'd already been gang raped by you and your friends
when he stumbled across your stupid little game.

You mistakenly thought that everyone was just like you,
but Tyrone proved you wrong
when he refused your invitation to sample the merchandise
and to take whatever he wanted.

He did.

He whupped your ass
and said "If you ever touch him again,
I'll come back and do it all again."

I don't believe in violence
or revenge,
but I can't lie.

I smiled.

THE HALLELUJAH LIFE

Love And Other Humiliating Acts

Perhaps the most humiliating day of all
was the day you raped me
in front of your friends,
taunting me again and again
before inviting them to do whatever they wanted
for no other reason than it gave you something to do.

They grabbed whatever objects their forever
blood-stained hands could find
and mutilated the very essence of my being
while you stood back taking pictures for your scrapbook.

When they were gone,
you said "I love you"
and for some reason I believed you.

Richard Propes

Storytellers

Every scar has its own special story,
from the burn marks on my shoulders and thighs
where you would taunt me
and tease me
while you penetrated me
late at night
in the upstairs closet
to the scratch marks
left from the dull end
of your broken refrigerator handle
when you stuck it up my ass
and laughed when you saw how much would fit inside me.

When I make love,
I find myself having to explain
each scar
over and over
and over again
and I find myself increasingly tired
of explaining
the varied ways you found to mutilate my body
and destroy my ability to make love
without these violent images raging inside my mind
as my lover tries desperately to love me.

Truth or Dare

Truth or dare.
Rape.

Sleepover.
Rape.

Bathing.
Rape.

Church.
Rape.

Gang.
Rape.

The closet.
Rape.

The woods.
Rape.

The party.
Rape.

I love you.
Rape.

Everything you said. Everything you did.
Rape.

Richard Propes

The Scripture That Ruined My Childhood

"Thou shalt not lie with mankind as with womankind;
it is an abomination."

"Do you know what this means, Richard?"

Silence.

"This means YOU are an abomination in the eyes of God,"
the elders who would serve as my judge and jury
pronounced with absolute certainty.

"Your mother shared with us
 that you were seen naked on a porch
with another boy."

"Is that true?"

Silence. They weren't listening anyway.

I wanted to scream, but I couldn't.

Why?

I wanted to plead, but I couldn't.

Why?

I wanted to speak my truth, but I couldn't.

Why?

"We have no choice, Richard."

"You can no longer participate in ministry school."

"You can come to church, but no one will be allowed to speak to you."

"You may not participate in activities with the other children."

"Do you understand, Richard?"

I wanted to scream out "No, I don't understand. I don't understand how you can be so stupid and so ignorant and so blind and so wrong."

I wanted to scream out "I'm 11-years-old and I don't understand any of this and I just want someone to explain this to me and try to understand what's going on inside of me."

But, I couldn't.

Richard Propes

A Reflection on Sexual Abuse

In his book "End of Memory," theologian Miroslav Volf talks about the concept of "remembering rightly." The essence of "remembering rightly" is both incredibly simple and mind-bogglingly complex. In my life, it means refusing to buy into my identity as a victim or survivor of sexual abuse. As Volf would put it "I am a beloved child of God."

It's that simple. "Remembering rightly" doesn't take away the abuse or the memories or the flashbacks or the ways in which enduring such violence impacted my life, but it allows me to even go beyond transcending the experiences into the realm of viewing the experiences through the eyes of God.

This doesn't mean there is some divine purpose behind sexual abuse or any form of abuse. There isn't. Abuse is never of God's will for us, regardless of the lessons we may take from it. I've always viewed arguments justifying abuse as misguided theological babble that only serve to minimize the suffering of humanity and the love of God. I don't believe there's a reason for child abuse, sexual abuse, domestic violence, poverty, crime, hunger, disability or any other of life's traumatic challenges or experiences.

Jeff, my perpetrator, tried in vain to ruin me for others. He repeated quite often that he wanted to leave me so damaged that no other human being would ever want me.

The most difficult thing to reconcile is, in fact, that Jeff did do permanent physical damage that continues to impact my life both in terms of function and in sexual performance.

Jeff would intentionally burn my genitals stating there was no use in their growing because no one would ever love me anyway. He would say time and again that, on the offbeat chance anyone else would ever want to have sex with me, that they would get me naked and then laugh.

Jeff would use various objects for penetration, acts and objects that resulted in permanent scars and impaired body function.

Whenever we were on his patio, Jeff would slam my face against the concrete with the stated goal of permanently disfiguring me. Having been born with hydrocephalus, or "water on the brain," I already possessed a slightly misshaped head but Jeff's physical abuse led to at least two permanent facial scars and severely crooked teeth.

For years, I couldn't look in a mirror without thinking about Jeff and abuse and rape and violence.

As I journeyed further into my healing process, and especially after becoming familiar with Miroslav Volf's life-changing work in the areas of theology and trauma, I began to realize that in order to truly manifest healing in my life I needed to change my identity.

I needed to "remember rightly." I needed to remember that I am a beloved child of God, an identity that rises above the scars, the traumatic life experiences, the dramas, the losses and/or the failures along the way.

This doesn't mean, by the way, that a simple shift of attitude was enough. Boy, I wish it would have been that easy. I literally went through a process of stripping away the old definitions and messages in my life and set out to find new ways to define such basic concepts as love, family, friendship, intimacy, sex and much more.

I have learned over the years that "remembering rightly" has a sacred place squarely in the foundation of healing and it has helped me overcome years of poor choices, self-destructive behaviors, suicide attempts, substance abuse and unhealthy relationships.

The more I believe myself to be a beloved child of God, the more I treat myself and others in a manner worthy of a child of God.

A Reflection on The Church

I have always loved the story that I shared earlier in this collection about my mother. When my mother, a lifelong Catholic, had a priest who suggested that perhaps she should let me die, she instead left Catholicism.

It had failed her. I know. I know. Not a huge surprise.

That's not a slam on Catholicism, but a slam on organized religion in general. I'm convinced that Jesus knew that organizing religion was a bad idea, because the more we organize the less we seem to individualize. My mother's priest had this huge collection of theological statements, principles and policies. What he'd failed to remember is that our God is the God of the "least of these." If this priest had managed to share God's love with my mother during this time, even if I had died she'd likely have remained a Catholic to this day.

Unfortunately, when Catholicism failed her my mother turned to Jehovah's Witnesses.

You know the JW's? The door knockers? The ones who don't celebrate birthdays or Christmas or, well, much of anything? The ones who don't say the "Pledge of Allegiance?" The ones who refuse blood transfusions and believe that only 144,000 will make it to heaven while the rest of the otherwise good folks will live in paradise on earth?

Yeah, them.

I've never quite understood how my fairly progressive, Democrat-voting mother who'd worked on the Robert F. Kennedy Jr. presidential campaign found herself convinced that the ultra-conservative Jehovah's Witnesses represented the path to her spiritual salvation. But hey, I spent time in the Vineyard Christian Fellowship. We all make mistakes.

I delivered my first sermon with Jehovah's Witnesses at the age of eight-years-old, a gripping five-minute piece on the story of David vs. Goliath that left them weeping.

I'm exaggerating.

I loved going to the Kingdom Hall. We attended church three times a week, though I've always felt like at least part of my mother's goal was to get away from an otherwise stressful and occasionally abusive home environment. I had Ministry School on Tuesdays, Bible Study on Thursdays and, of course, every Sunday morning.

Again, I loved it. I recognized early on that I didn't always agree with their theology, but the Jehovah's Witnesses were my family and I adored everyone in the Guion Creek Congregation.

Some of my best childhood memories involve my mother and I, my father did not attend due to an incident of being "talked about" because of his casual dress, as we attended church conferences throughout the Midwest.

Jehovah's Witnesses didn't so much have traditional ministers as they did have "Elders." The "Elders" were the spiritual leaders of the local congregation and essentially served as a collective of pastors locally and in larger district roles. There was no traditional pastoral role and, with the exception of Ministry School, no formal training that I could ever identify other than being identified as a good, obedient JW.

I had every intention of giving my life to God even from a young age. While I never became baptized with the Jehovah's Witnesses, I had already identified as a young boy that ministry was where I felt called. Since I had a serious physical disability with serious physical limitations, a lot of the traditional school activities were considered off limits. This was still the 70's and 80's, so disability stereotypes were prevalent and I was even banned from the class Industrial Arts in favor of Home Economics because Industrial Arts was considered too risky and unsafe.

The church was my life.

I was regarded as a gifted preacher at a young age, and the Elders in my congregation often marveled at my ability to comprehend even complex scriptural passages. While my interpretation occasionally conflicted with their own understandings, I was respected for my ability to make scripture more accessible.

I was seriously reprimanded once for including a political reference in a Thursday evening message that paralleled the dysfunctional behavior of church leadership during the times of Jesus. Among the many things JW's discouraged was political involvement, because there was only one King to whom they surrendered.

The parallel was legit. I was right.

I have always had a love/hate relationship with organized religion. Actually, more precisely, I could probably say "I love God, but despise organized religion." It's not so much that I've never experienced an organized religious body that actually followed the teachings of Jesus or Buddha or Muhammad but, well, it has been very seldom that I've experienced such a church.

It seems like most people believe that God should be made in their image rather than the other way around.

My unhealthy relationship with organized religion certainly started with Jehovah's Witnesses, but I've always been a bit of a spiritual seeker and have had some remarkably interesting, dysfunctional and occasionally abusive experiences with the likes of Vineyard Christian Fellowship, Christian & Missionary Alliance, Unitarian-Universalist, New Age, Unity, Pentecostal and others. Some of these experiences have proven to be quite positive, and along the way I've met extraordinary spiritual seekers like myself. Some of these seekers, even in my most fundamental detours, remain beloved friends and peers to this day.

I've often wondered how the two church elders I met with, Steve and Howard, would have responded had I been able to find my voice when confronted by them over my alleged "homosexual behavior" with Jeff.

Would they have been compassionate?

Would they have understood?

Would they have reported the abuse or would they have stood firm on their tunnel-vision interpretation that it was "homosexual behavior?"

Would my life have gone a completely different direction? I've always believed that my lack of truth-telling was based in my own fear and an awareness of the reality of life within the conservative Jehovah's Witnesses. I would learn years later of an alleged pattern of JW's circumventing the required reporting of child sexual abuse, a not exactly uncommon trait of organized religious bodies across many denominations.

I've also wondered if, perhaps, I carried more than a smidgen of guilt that I did spend years believing that Jeff loved me and just didn't know how to express it. It took me years to identify his behavior as abusive, and in that failure to identify abuse I certainly had to acknowledge that there were aspects of the abuse I enjoyed and appreciated.

I'd never really heard the words "I love you" before. Jeff said "I love you" all the time. Even though he followed up his words with physical and sexual abuse, hearing the words was somehow really meaningful for me at the time. I craved the words "I love you."

Jeff may have hurt my body, actually he did hurt my body, but he also wasn't afraid of it. With the exception of nurses during my many hospitalizations, there was very little tenderness or affection in my life and I'm very aware that I craved human contact and appreciation for my physical being.

I craved touch that didn't involve surgery or medical procedures or shots or needles or catheters or anal probing, though I suppose I still ended up with the anal probing, eh?

I was only 11-years-old by the time my sexual abuse from Jeff was winding down, but if enjoying having a boy touch me meant I was gay then I was fine with that conclusion being reached.

After it was concluded by the elders that I was exhibiting homosexual tendencies, the decision was made that I would be shunned by the congregation and removed from Ministry School.

I was devastated, but tried to maintain my relationship with Jehovah's Witnesses for another year or two out of both rebelliousness and dependence. Ultimately, I would leave the path behind unclear on whether I had been rejected by the church or God or both.

In a wee bit of dark irony, my mother would also eventually be what the JW's call "disfellowshipped." In her case, because she was baptized, her failure to quit smoking led to her discipline by the church body.

I learned many good things throughout my childhood with Jehovah's Witnesses, especially about the importance of family. While they ultimately failed to share God's love with me and with my mother during our times of need, they helped me begin the journey of exploring my own relationship with God rather than allowing it to be defined by the beliefs and actions of others.

I struggled with the question "Had God abandoned me in my hour of need?," but in the end wrestled even more with the idea that during this darkest period of my life perhaps something I had done had made the God I'd always worshipped with reckless abandon somehow hate me.

The Question That Can't Be Answered

Why?

Why did I stay?

Why did I keep going back even after the abuse intensified?

There is no question that spina bifida opened the door to my abuse, but it did not cause it.

Jeff is responsible.

There is no question that my overwhelming loneliness contributed, even at the age of eleven, to my sense of social desperation.

But, loneliness did not cause my abuse.

Jeff is responsible.

There is no question that my teachers weren't paying attention.

I smelled.
My grades dropped.
I isolated.
In short, I changed. Drastically.

But, my teachers did not cause my abuse.

Jeff is responsible.

There is no question that my home life was troubled, but my parents did not cause my sexual abuse.

Jeff is responsible.

I was lonely. I was desperate. I was insecure. I was disabled.

But, Jeff is responsible.

Richard Propes

Flashbacks

I remember the blond hair on his hands
reaching between my legs
and his baby smooth stomach
with a thin line of hair
leading down his torso
towards his constantly erect penis.

I remember craving him when he was gone
because of the love
and affection
and trust
and comfort he provided.

I remember
going down on him
and the smile on his face
when I could put all of his manhood
in my mouth and swallow.

I remember feeling lucky
he loved me
and didn't laugh
at my body
disabled since birth.

I got lost for awhile
and truly believed
in the wondrous blessings of his love.

Imaginary Crimes

I have destroyed
the hopes and dreams of every living soul.

I have robbed the broken
and ravaged their faith and vision.

I have raped the lover by my side
with every single word and touch.

Every breath I take
is a crime against humanity.

Everything I see
is covered with blood.

I bind myself in shame
for the crimes you do not see.

I will never touch you.
I will never speak to you.
I will never look at you.
I will never hurt you.

I will never.

Richard Propes

Connection

I have been told by my therapist
that an individual is supposed to learn
how to connect with another human being
as a child
and continue
developing those skills throughout life.

I don't recall ever feeling connected
to my parents
or my church
or anyone else in my childhood
and I vividly recall
significant periods
when I felt so alone
that I would have done anything
just to feel connected.

At five-years-old,
I learned how to fake an orgasm
smile for the camera
and connect with a girl
by sticking my penis into her vagina
and telling her she was sexy
even though I wasn't really sure what sexy meant.

By twelve-years-old,
I had learned to connect
with groups of people
by perfecting the art of a blow job
and allowing them to penetrate me
whenever
and wherever
they so desired.

THE HALLELUJAH LIFE

By the time I was a teenager,
I no longer had a desire for connection
and locked myself away
and became frightened of the world outside.

By my early twenties,
I was even more isolated
after my wife committed suicide
and killed our newborn child
and I started living in my car
and selling myself when I could
but I finally decided I really couldn't sell myself
so I dabbled with drugs
and spent several years trying to kill myself.

By my thirties,
I began to discover the truth
that there were good people in the world
who would love me "as is"
without the violence
and the rage
and the sex
and the manipulation
and the pain.

I am in my forties now,
and I don't remember the last time I got laid
but I know without a doubt that I am
loved
deeply loved
every moment
of every day
of my life.

A Reflection on Valerie

Third grade.

It was in third grade that Valerie and I became friends while attending Central Elementary School.

Have you ever met someone with whom you just "clicked?"

Valerie and I were remarkably different, but our personalities seemed to complement one another almost perfectly.

She was intelligent, kind, just a wee bit goofy and she had grown up around a hearing impaired grandmother so disability didn't seem to bother her.

In fact, I can't really remember a time when she ever used the word "disability" in any of our conversations.

From an early age, Valerie and I seemed to exist on the fringes of social acceptance within our school.

Valerie was always just a tad different from everyone else, a difference that I found refreshing but a difference that pretty much assured her existence in the outer circle of the high school experience.

To be honest, she preferred it that way anyway.

I was sort of my school's token gimp. With the exception of my experiences with Jeff, I received only a modest amount of teasing and taunting. I was one of the few students with disabilities who was never in a special education class, a fact that allowed me to enjoy a more inclusive high school experience. However, I was remarkably different even before the impact of my abuse really set in.

I suppose if I had to use a word for it, I'd say that I was "appreciated." I never went to parties, never really had friends, never dated and never really even hung out much with more than a small handful of people. But, I seemed to enjoy the admiration of my peers in a way that was never condescending.

I was an average student for whom high school became a bit of a sanctuary thanks to the abundant opportunities in writing and public speaking. I served on my school's yearbook and newspaper staffs, while also competing on the Speech Team all four years of high school.

There's a photo of me in my high school yearbook giving a speech about skateboarding and, yes, there I was on my crutches riding a skateboard down the halls of good ole' Pike High School.

From middle school on, Valerie and I were known as friends. There were some who were surprised that we didn't end up together, but our friendship wasn't about chemistry or sparks or romance. It was about respect, intelligence, compassion for others and a largely unspoken admiration for one another.

Think about it.

Valerie's friendship has never wavered.

I can't tell you the number of times she's visited me in hospitals during middle school and high school. She lives thousands of miles away now in Baltimore, but without failure if she sees a social networking post that concerns her I'll end up with a message, e-mail or voice-mail.

It was during fifth or sixth grade that we started sitting by each other on the bus, and we did so until we graduated from high school. Even when she started driving, she would often join me on the bus or I would join her in her car.

She never knew about the sexual abuse, at least not until I first started speaking out in my early twenties. She did, however, deal patiently and compassionately with my poor self-care (I stunk!) and my occasionally erratic behavior.

I was secretly devastated when she went away to college at Purdue University, a relatively short trip from Indianapolis that felt like it was so far away. She had been my emotional anchor during high school, a truth that may or may not surprise her.

She performed in a play I wrote called "Laughter in the Rain," a play about abuse/suicide that was so intense that some seriously wondered if I planned to kill myself at the end of the show.

Basically, when it comes down to it, she has loved and respected me for 35+ years through life's many peaks and valleys.

I was a groomsman in her wedding, and she stood by that choice even after my heavy drinking and chaotic emotions threatened to derail my attendance at her wedding.

The most overwhelming moment was the day that she and her husband asked me to be a godparent for their daughter, Victoria.

It was this moment that changed my life forever. Becoming a godparent and accepting responsibility for the future of a child forced me to live a better, healthier life and to become the human being that Valerie obviously believed me to be.

We're both in our forties now, and I seldom go a month without getting an e-mail suggesting that I move to the east coast where she now lives.

After 35+ years, we seldom go more than a week without an e-mail or phone call.

Valerie has also been one of the people who has been a constant reminder that it's not always about the person who says "I love you" all the time, but about the person who actually does love you all the time.

She's extraordinary.

When I start contemplating my life's hallelujah moments, Valerie is always at the top of the list.

Intimate High School Secrets

I remember peeing.
A lot.

My life was simple really.

Wake up early.
Bathe. I hated touching myself.
Go to school.

Three out of five days, maybe more, the ostomy bag would spring a leak while at school.

Piss-stained polyester pants.

Do you wonder why I had no friends?

I remember walking up to receive an award during Senior Awards Day and feeling the familiar dripping as my ostomy bag sprung a leak at precisely the most humiliating time.

Did anyone know? I have no idea.

I did.

I didn't date. I know. I know. Big surprise.

I first started contemplating suicide in my junior year of high school, going so far as to begin competing in Original Oratory with a speech about suicide prevention.

I've always had a dark sense of humor.

It was required to survive high school.

Richard Propes

The First Suicide Attempt

The simple truth is that no one expected me to survive.

I wasn't taught to live life as an independent adult, so when my father's employer offered me my first post-high school job experience it really was destined to fail.

After all, who really thought that a paraplegic on crutches could work construction?

Labor work? Yeah, right.

Receptionist? The other receptionist seemed to have a problem with the occasional piss stains she'd encounter when following my shift.

Go figure.

Job secretary? Okay, well, at least being dirty all the time didn't seem to matter much.

After a year, there was a "mutual" (i.e., I was let go) decision that it simply wasn't working out.

I had longed for most of my young life to have an experience in which my father and I could bond.

He went out on a limb to get me the job, and I failed. Miserably.

It wasn't so much the failure as it was the humiliating way in which I failed that was so devastating.

After all, how many people really lose a job because they can't stay clean or stop peeing everywhere?

I felt worthless. I felt disgusting.

I went home, grabbed a loaded .45 and put it to my head. Before I could pull the trigger, the sounds of John Hiatt's "Have A Little Faith In Me" started playing on the radio.

"There is no way that's a sign," I thought to myself.

I sat there listening to the lyrics
while weeping profusely.

I put the gun down.

I would learn years later that Hiatt wrote the song for his daughter after the suicide his wife and her mother.

Richard Propes

Secret Heart

There is one secret
I have never told anyone.

I want to be held...

gently

touched
rocked
nurtured

not
like a child
but
like a man

who simply wants to be loved.

In a safe place,
I want to learn to trust.

I want someone
to understand
my needs
respect
my body
embrace
my soul.

I want to know
that I can be loved.

The Therapist

We would sit in her office on the second floor
of the antiquated downtown building,
pictures of her children on her desk
the windows cracked ever so slightly
to allow breathing room amidst the stench
of my poorly cared for body and disintegrating soul.

Invariably, when I was her last appointment of the evening,
her husband would be anxiously awaiting her arrival
through the double doors signifying the end
of yet another extended session.

With the gentle spirit
of an angel she would quietly soothe me
while listening,
sometimes for hours,
as I cried
and screamed
of the horrors being relived in my mind.

Wearing gloves so I wouldn't be frightened,
she touched me
softly
and learned how to reach me
and nurture me
in a way that felt safer
than I'd ever felt.

We could spend the entire session,
me in one corner of her office
trying desperately to work up the courage
to touch fingertips
so that I could connect with another human being.

She brought me out of my shell
into a world
instantly frightening
yet, oh so, fascinating.

There were times she sang to me
and times she talked for hours ...
times she would touch me
hold me
comfort me
protect me
from the violence raging inside my mind.

I trusted her
with the most fragile parts of my inner being
and rejoiced in the miracle of childlike discovery
and wonder.

Then we kissed.

I felt at peace with myself
for the first time in my life,
and began to believe that,
perhaps,
I could experience the feelings
I had never dared to dream.

My body felt loved.
My soul felt secure.

We made love. Or had sex. Or fucked.

The therapist went away
replaced by a mother
and a lover ...
still loving
caring and nurturing...

yet, everything was different,
somehow different.

For years,
everything felt right even though everything was a lie.
Her passionate embrace surpassed
everything I had ever experienced,
her acceptance a healing balm
for a wounded body and soul.

Words could never express the joy I found
in learning how to love another human being ...
offering her the vulnerability
of my life
my love
and my newly discovered hope and innocence.

I knew, on some level, that this "love" was not "right,"
but I vowed to protect her
and to never tell our secret.

Yet, something inside me still ached.

Life evolved.
Healing became quietly sacrificed.

Like a child, my faith in her never wavered.
Like a child, I believed in her
trusted her
and refused to believe that I had fallen once again
for a love impure.

Questions created chaos
in my heart and quietly
I lost my faith
convinced the truth had revealed itself once again.

Fingertips
became daggers piercing my heart.

I went numb knowing
that everything was true except for the lies
and that I would never again feel loved
never again feel desired
with this body
so beaten and scarred
bruised and burned
violated beyond recognition.

I said goodbye to the therapist
and goodbye to the hopes and dreams and visions
she helped create.

Torn between
shame and rage
grief and joy
peace and chaos ...

I have searched for meaning in a relationship
that gave birth to my affirmation of life,
yet, tragically met its end through the questions
only a love built on the miracle of true childlike discovery
and wonder can ever begin to answer.

I still believe.

A Reflection on The Therapist

She saved my life.

I was caught up in a self-destructive, suicidal perfect storm when I crossed paths with the woman who would serve as my therapist for four years while being my lover for nearly three of those years. Her actions, our actions, violated every professional boundary and yet, simultaneously, her actions and risk-taking and vulnerability very likely saved my life.

Could she have achieved so much positive without violating professional boundaries? It's hard to say, but I do know that therapists before her failed miserably in addressing the flashbacks, preventing the self-destructive behaviors and ending the suicidal ideation. While she certainly does not deserve all the credit for my turn-around (I do!), there's simply no doubt in my mind that her willingness to adapt the therapeutic journey to my comprehensive needs was a major factor in my becoming a healthier adult.

The "relationship" began after a temporary loss of my driver's license led to our therapeutic sessions becoming home-based sessions. We'd been working on touch issues and, in retrospect, such therapeutic issues simply weren't safe in the home-based setting.

The relationship started to sour after I served an internship on an inpatient psychiatric unit as I neared college graduation. Thrust into the role of counselor, I began to realize how incredibly wrong and unhealthy our relationship was and exactly why the therapeutic relationship does require professional boundaries. Despite my mixed feelings about losing someone who'd been so central to my healing, I requested an end to the physical aspects of our relationship.

She had always believed that I would someday move on. She believed, or at least stated she believed, that she was preparing me for a healthy relationship and to move on with my life. However, when I did finally decided to cut off all contact with her, I could feel the realness of her feelings and the hurt she was experiencing.

I entered what would prove to be a short-lived relationship/engagement, but I knew I could never do so while hanging on to my therapist/lover/best friend.

I have only updated the poem that precedes this reflection, a poem that I first published in my "Imaginary Crimes" collection of poetry. I watched as she bought the collection at a conference we both attended, but we have never again spoken about the events of the past.

I regret, in most ways, the direction that our relationship took yet I cannot bring myself to regret the relationship itself. I am saddened that our relationship is marred by secrets that cannot be spoken and boundaries that were violated, yet I remain grateful for the many ways in which she taught me how to touch, how to love, how to be vulnerable and how to, in the end, make the healthiest choice possible for my life.

Healing Is

recognizing that I don't deserve to be
hurt
verbally
physically
sexually
emotionally
spiritually.

Healing is
restoring my spirit
my faith
my belief
in myself and others
as well as
my capacity
to be human
and experience joy
and childlike wonder.

Healing is a process
that cannot be manipulated
to fit the needs
of my therapist
my family
or my abuser.

Healing is a lifelong commitment to myself
and a willingness to experience
my shame
and risk
my trust
time and time again.

Healing is the recognition
my scars are deep
and will come back to me
throughout the years
in my joys
and in my sorrows
sometimes
taking me back to the days
when I was a young child
cowering in the corner of my closet.

Healing is the confession of my memories
to myself and others,
even the most shameful parts
of my personal history.

Healing is the conscious return to life
the memories I fought for years to destroy.

Healing is playing
with the essence of my being
and putting together
pieces of a puzzle
with no clue what the final result
will even look like.

Healing is grieving
immense losses I have experienced
and acknowledging that which might have been
may never be.

Healing is learning how to be nurtured
and surrounding myself with those I trust
and who are safe
so I can be vulnerable enough
to discover the strength I truly possess.

Healing is breaking the cycle
by acting on my own truth
and erasing the messages
of my perpetrator
by embracing my journey
and fearlessly walking towards freedom.

Healing is feeling
all my feelings
despite the hurt
the contradiction
the overwhelm
and the loss of control.

Healing is loyalty
to myself
and freedom
from years of undeserved bondage
to my abuser.

Healing is a return to innocence
through listening
to the child within
and finding
hearing
believing
this child.

Healing is trusting myself
enough to know that I will find my way home
and need never be alone.

Healing is knowing
I deserve
to be loved
to be held

to be accepted
to be believed
to be heard
to be respected
to be celebrated.

Healing is becoming proud of being the man that I am
and learning how to define masculinity in a way that honors me.

Healing is my way of acknowledging
I am special
I am wonderful
I am beautiful
I am priceless in my existence
I am that which I've always dreamed I'd become.

A Confession

I have a confession. I love airport scenes in movies. You know the ones I'm talking about? Sometimes, it seems like they're in every romantic comedy or romantic drama around. The storyline is always simple - man and woman fall in love, man and woman fall apart and man races to the airport to confess his love.

I love these scenes.

I think I most love the idea of racing for the ones we love. I love the image of a man or woman running through the airport determined to not let go of the one they love. It can be a completely comical scene and it will inevitably bring me to tears.

This is also how I picture my relationship with God. I screw up and we have a nasty break-up where I say some really awful things. I realize my mistakes and inevitably find myself racing back to a God who always welcomes me back with open arms.

Richard Propes

Voluntary Virginity

The simple truth is I started losing my virginity at the age of five, and had fully lost it by the age of nine.

I didn't choose to do so, but that doesn't matter.

By the age of nine-years-old, my innocence was gone.

I understood sex, maybe not fully but enough to know that I could use sex to survive a horrific situation.

I understood that if I performed well, I could avoid the burnings or the beatings or the humiliation.

Maybe not always, but much of the time this was true.

So, I performed and I survived.

Of course, by the time it came to actually have sex voluntarily I'd forgotten almost everything I'd already learned.

Sex is not like riding a bicycle.

THE HALLELUJAH LIFE

There are People in Life Who Cannot Be Loved

It was resting comfortably
underneath a months old pile of beer cans
between the teddy bear she'd left for me to remember her by
and her favorite pair of panties that I'm guessing she just forgot.

"There are people in life who cannot be loved and
you are one of the nicest..."

That's it.
Nothing else.

There was no "I'm leaving you and will never be back."

There was no "I hate you" or "Fuck you" or "I wish you were dead."

An incomplete note.
A teddy bear.
And panties.

I met Laura in an emergency room, where she was being treated for a sexually transmitted disease.

Trust me. I can't make this shit up.

We both came from horrid backgrounds, but wanted a better life and we found it with each other.

She stopped stripping.

I stopped drinking. Mostly.

She was beautiful and kind and very, very funny. She was way out of my league.

She said "You're the first guy who didn't try to fuck me on the first date."

I guess that was a good thing.

We married on the way to Vegas. Long story. Bad idea.

One night, she announced she wanted to go visit family in Dallas.
"I'll be back," she promised.
As if to reassure me, we spent the evening
having the most glorious conversations
about our future.

We talked about children,
though both of us had said we'd never want them.

"If we had a daughter, what would you want to name her?,"
she inquired innocently enough.

"Jennifer?"

"Jennifer Lynn," I responded.
"She would have to have your middle name."

She did.

THE HALLELUJAH LIFE

A Letter to Jennifer

Dear Jennifer,

You don't know me, but I'm your father.

I don't know how it's possible to miss someone you've never met, but I do. There isn't a day that goes by that you don't cross my mind.

In one breath, I think to myself I would have been such a horrible father. Then, in the next breath I find myself wishing I'd just gotten the chance to try. I wouldn't have been perfect. I know that.

But, I would have tried. I would have loved you. I know that. I absolutely know that. I would have given you everything I had, even though I've never had much.

I often wonder if you'd have grown up loving me, or if I'd have been that godawful parent who sends their child into therapy for the rest of their life.

Sorry seems like such a stupid word, but I am sorry. Every single day of my life since I learned about you, I've been sorry.

I'm sorry I wasn't there when you were born.

I'm sorry I wasn't there when you died.

I'm sorry I didn't read between the lines and know what your mother was trying to tell me. I'm sorry I let her leave.

I'm so sorry I let her hurt you.

I'm so sorry I didn't stop her - that I didn't do something.

I don't know where you are. I'm not sure I believe in heaven or hell or anything like that, but wherever you are I really hope you don't hate me and I really hope you don't hate your mother.

I swear she didn't hate you. She didn't mean for you to die. She was just scared. She would have loved you if she'd have only figured out how.

We didn't want to be parents, but that doesn't mean we wouldn't have loved you. We were just terrified that we would do something horribly, horribly wrong.

I have this strange feeling you've been with me for years. Maybe that's just wishful thinking, but I feel your presence and it's a really, really good thing.

I have a feeling you would have been a daddy's girl, but even using the word daddy feels wrong because I didn't protect you.

I used to think that maybe you were better off not growing up with us as your parents, but nowadays I can't help but think you'd have turned into a really amazing young woman.

All I can say is that I love you and I would have loved you. I would have poured everything I had into loving you. I would have been scared out of my mind, but I would not have failed you.

I pray that wherever you are now that you're at peace. You deserve peace. If you ever see your mother, please tell her I forgive her.

Really.

I love you.

THE HALLELUJAH LIFE

A Reflection on Jennifer and Fatherhood

The story that I had been told for several years was that my wife of less than one year, Laura, had killed herself while visiting family in Dallas. Because she had been so open with her family about our marital struggles, I was not welcome at the funeral and was left to grieve on my own.

Not long after her funeral, I received word that she had been pregnant when she passed away.

Then, a random search of a genealogy site unexpectedly revealed the truth that would ultimately be confirmed by Laura's surviving family in a rather uncomfortable Christmas Eve confrontation.

Jennifer Lynn Propes had been born and died under "suspicious circumstances" not long after birth. My wife, who had struggled for years with mental illness and addiction, then killed herself.

Having already been extensively lied to by my wife's family, I set out to research her death myself and hired a private investigator. I confirmed that, for the most part, everything I'd been told this time was actually true.

So, while my daughter died just over twenty years ago, it has only been in the last five years that the truth of her life and death were revealed to me.

I remember the sheer horror I felt while in my twenties and contemplating the possibility of fatherhood. I was absolutely convinced that my child would become the next serial killer or front page evildoer. In addition to what felt like an incredibly dysfunctional family tree, I simply had no concept of normal developmental growth and believed that I would do irreparable harm by becoming a father. In essence, my ultimate act of showing how much I cared about children was to make sure I never had one of my own.

In addition to my long-standing diagnosis of Post-Traumatic Stress Disorder from my childhood sexual abuse, I had been assigned the diagnosis of Reactive Attachment Disorder. It was my diagnosis of Reactive Attachment Disorder (RAD) that led my therapist to such extraordinary lengths in an effort to better normalize the experience of human bonding in my life. When I found myself contemplating parenting or becoming a foster parent or even when I once considered adoption, I always found myself asking the question "What if I can't bond with my own child?"

Trapped

My telephone was disconnected again yesterday.
My apartment is a mess
and I don't have the energy to clean.

I live here in this self-designed
especially secure
deluxe-model
prison.

Isolation
makes love to me
daily
enveloping me
daily
as I grow more frightened
of the love
that I so strongly desire.

Yet
I remain loyal
to my old voices
as the prison door
slams shut
day
after
day
after
day
after
day
after
day...

One Last Suicide Attempt

Over a five year period, I had three serious suicide attempts and numerous suicidal gestures.

In case you're wondering, I never succeeded.

Most of my attempts were mild, casual gestures serving more as attention-seeking behaviors than anything. Over the course of the year following the death of my wife and, at the time I believed, unborn child, I would lose virtually everything a human being can lose.

In addition to the loss of my wife and child, I found myself in a downward spiral that led to a complete financial collapse and a period of homelessness or, in my case, living in my car. Finally, my poor self-care complicated my already fragile health situation and over the course of a year both of my feet were amputated below the knees due to severe infections.

I had been kicked out of yet another church, the Vineyard Christian Fellowship, because of my self-destructive patterns. With literally nothing to my name and having lost my church family once again, I concluded that this was God's sign that suicide was okay.

I know. Poor logic, but I was depressed. What'd you expect?

During this time, I picked up the semi-amusing habit of creating an actual calendar with detailed information on what days and what times I could call certain members of my support system and how long I would be able to talk to them before they would burn out. I also became a regular caller to the local crisis intervention hotline, though my incredibly unresolved issues with men would frequently lead me to hang up if the person on the other end happened to be male.

I may have been suicidal, but I had a really dark sense of humor.

Taking everything I had with me, I drove to the parking lot of a local supermarket on the Westside of Indianapolis and parked my car. I called no one, I left no notes and I proceeded to dowse my

Chevy Cavalier in gasoline. Just for good measure, I also dowsed my clothing in gasoline.

I mean dowse.

I climbed into the backseat of the car, prayed what I believed to be a fairly useless prayer for some sort of sign that this wasn't the right answer and, just for old time's sake, popped in my John Hiatt's "Bring the Family" CD just in case God wanted to produce yet another offbeat miracle in my life.

Then, I closed my eyes and pulled out a lighter. I placed the burning flame directly on the gasoline that had been used to dowse my car.

Get that?

I placed the burning flame directly on the gasoline.

Explosion, right? Obviously? Um. Nothing. There was no smoldering. No spark. No fire. No explosion.

I was pissed.

I did it again. And again. And again. And again. I sat there. Stunned. I climbed out of my vehicle, mainly because the smell was starting to bother me and clearly I'd done something wrong.

I did the only thing I knew to do at that point. I called my therapist.

"You did what?"

"Um. Well. I tried to blow up my car with me in it?"

"Are you stupid?"

"You're the one having an affair with me. Where does that put you?"

"Why would you call me AFTER?"

"Well, I didn't want to call you before. That seemed cruel."

About that time, I looked over my shoulder and, just to make sure I was listening, God had placed in front of me an old friend and the former editor of my college newspaper.

"Richard?"

I tried being nonchalant.

This is not easy when you smell like gasoline and are really just praying that the person you're speaking with isn't a smoker.

That would have been really ironic.

"Um, hey there! How are you?"

I've always believed Leslie, with whom I am still friends, knew exactly what was going on even if it was only in her subconscious. I quickly said goodbye to my therapist and returned to my conversation with Leslie. I didn't reveal the morbid details of my behavior, but I shared more than enough for her to realize that I was in a downward spiral.

She offered me a writing job with a local newspaper, a place to stay for the night and a meal.

How many of you have ever gotten a job offer while dowsed in gasoline?

Okay, God. I'm listening.

A Reflection on Suicide

When most of my friends discover the intimate details of my past, the one thing that most surprises them is that I have attempted suicide and truly struggled for years with suicidal ideation.

I'm almost universally regarded and recognized by my friends as an optimistic, happy and loving person with a perpetual smile on my face.

The weird thing is that the smile has never been fake.

I learned fairly early on that it was possible to be both suicidal and "happy." My suicidal feelings weren't borne out of some miserable depression or unrelenting darkness. My suicidal feelings were, first and foremost, about a sense of loneliness that couldn't be satisfied and physical and emotional feelings that I simply could not get under control.

My life has always been dramatic. I mean, c'mon, I made the front page of my local newspaper at birth. I popped out of my mother ass first and with a hole in my spine. I spent my first several weeks of life living in a full body cast, and spent a good majority of my childhood hospitalized and experiencing over 50+ surgeries.

I'm not even going to talk about the sexual abuse again.

My life was always intense and dramatic. I think, on a certain level, I was terrified of normalcy.

I'm not even sure that I was suicidal most of the time that I was popping pills or overdosing or cutting myself or burning myself.

The car dowsed in gasoline? Yeah, that was real. I was suicidal and I was royally ticked when it didn't work. Most of the time, I just really was trying to deal with the intensity of my emotions and I was failing miserably. I burned out friend after friend during this period in my life, most of whom were fairly fragile themselves and simply couldn't afford the risk of continuing to associate with someone so bent on self-abuse.

The first time I remember feeling love was with my friend Melissa, a fellow sexual abuse survivor whose healing was at least a bit ahead of my own and whose patience with me seemed endless. She was on my calendar of friends that I could call. The only other time I contemplated using a gun in a suicide attempt, Melissa intervened and literally took the gun from my hands while we were both sitting in her office at Riley Children's Hospital.

Suicide has always had a presence in my life. I suppose that's not really a surprise since part of the proceeds from this book are benefiting the Indiana Chapter of American Foundation for Suicide Prevention.

My first girlfriend? She killed herself.

My next girlfriend became my wife. She killed herself.

The next woman with whom I became engaged? You guessed it. She attempted suicide while we were engaged and eventually succeeded.

The list goes on and on. At one point during my suicidal days, I formed a "suicide club" with a group of four friends. I am the lone survivor. Yes, there is still survivor's guilt.

I found the body of one friend who'd shot himself in the head, and have dealt with suicide time and again with both friends and family.

There are some things I have learned along the way that I believe are important:

I can't save everyone, but I can love everyone. I'm amazed how often either giving or receiving a hug, a phone call, a kind word, a small gift, a compliment or simply a smile has made a difference.

If you're going to ask someone "How are you?," then stick around and listen for their answer. You're not doing anyone any good by asking the question if you don't actually care about the answer.

You need those friends who will just wrap you in their arms whether you ask for it or not. I still have days where my body relives the abuse so intensely that it's practically all I can feel. There are days when your phone call, your hand, your hug or your voice may make all the difference in the world.

You also need those friends who will hold back and realize that sometimes a hug isn't what's needed.

There's a scene in the movie "Lars and the Real Girl" where Ryan Gosling's character is waiting on news about his hospitalized "girlfriend." Four sewing circle ladies from his church have joined him. He's clearly unsure how to respond.

"Is there something I should be doing?," he asks.

"No, dear. You eat," says one.

"We came over to sit," says two.

"That's what people do when tragedy strikes," says three.

"They come over and sit," says four.

That's exactly it. We matter to each other. We matter to our friends, our family, our co-workers, our classmates and the strangers on the street. We matter to people in faraway lands whom we will never meet. A different therapist, one I didn't sleep with, once shared a story about driving along in her car having a horrible day when she looked over and the guy in the next vehicle gave her the biggest, most genuine smile. It completely changed the course of her day.

I'm convinced that the number one way to prevent suicide is to love one another. It doesn't always work, but it's a great place to start.

Richard Propes

The Beginning of Tenderness

It was October 8, 1989.

I was sitting in downtown Indianapolis in my wheelchair. I had a backpack on the wheelchair, twenty dollars in my pocket and a handful of press releases announcing my mission. I'd previously notified Prevent Child Abuse Indiana of my plans, but when I arrived at their doorsteps on Massachusetts Avenue I quickly discovered that they weren't even wheelchair accessible.

They also weren't downstairs waiting for me, likely a result of the fact that my plan was completely insane and they probably thought I wouldn't really go through with it.

But, there I was.

A few weeks earlier, I'd been trying to come up with a creative way that I could really truly discover for myself whether or not life was worth living. I wanted to figure out if there was anything resembling tenderness in the world. I'd tried a couple of smaller fund-raisers, including a poetry reading that raised $10 for the Marion County Mental Health Association and, in what really started my extreme activism, a 24-hour arts festival called the Compassion Street Arts Festival.

The arts festival had convinced me that I could really organize a special event. I'd convinced the owner of the Arlington Theatre, a local concert hall, to donate his space. He did so on one condition - I had to completely book all 24 hours of the arts festival AND they all had to show up.

I was joined by my longtime friend Victor, who served as my technical director, and I booked every hour on the hour. There was only one no show, and I had an act on standby ready to jump in.

The space was donated, and while the event wasn't an overwhelming success it did raise thousands of dollars for a local group of arts therapists who worked with survivors of sexual abuse. Every artist donated their time and talent, ranging from local faves like P.S. Dump Your Boyfriend and Ann McWilliams to high school bands, comics, soloists and so many more.

Heck, I even got engaged for the second time that night. That was definitely NOT a success.

So, as I was sitting with my friends we started toying around with words and phrases and ideas. I kept going back to the word "Tenderness," which also happened to be a song by the band General Public that I was really in love with at the time.

While it wasn't really a brilliant idea, my friend's wife came over beside me and began using a sewing needle to tattoo my arm with the word "tenderness." Though, if you look carefully, it actually looks like it says "tender mess."

Perfect.

So, I was sitting in downtown Indianapolis in my wheelchair wondering just what the heck I'd talked myself into.

The plan was simple but absurd. I was going to do what I was calling the "Tenderness Tour," a 41-day and 1,000 mile wheelchair ride around the border of Indiana with a couple zigzags tossed in for good measure.

I wasn't an athlete. I wasn't in great shape. I'd trained a bit, but nowhere near enough for something requiring endurance. I'd written all the local media to tell them of my plans and, when possible, had gone to the library to look up local contacts in each of the mapped out towns I would visit. On the day I left, I had places to stay scheduled in about a half dozen of the cities I would visit.

I had no clue what was going to happen, but I knew I was going through with it. After all, if I failed perhaps that would only prove my point that there were no good people in the world and I really was worthless. I had no money to fall back on, so if I didn't receive the kindness of strangers my trip would likely downward spiral quickly.

Once everyone at Prevent Child Abuse Indiana realized I was serious and already there, the entire office staff quickly scurried outside to greet me. They clearly thought I was insane, or maybe that was just me projecting.

Within five more minutes, my therapist arrived (Yeah, her!).

I prepared to start. While I was talking to the Prevent Child Abuse Indiana staff about my plans, I suddenly looked around and realized I was surrounded by television stations from WRTV, WTHR, WXIN and WISH.

I was surrounded by ALL the local television stations plus the local newspaper and even local radio stations.

I was amazed. I knew why I was doing the Tenderness Tour, but I had no clue how to communicate why I was doing it. I never imagined that anyone would ever pay attention to it.

I spent a few minutes talking with the local media, then I started wheeling towards my first day destination of Shelbyville, Indiana. Boy, that was bad planning on my part.

I did, however, make it to Greenfield, Indiana. In Greenfield, I was greeted by the city's fire chief who immediately offered me a place to stay for the evening plus a meal.

Wow. Kindness right off the bat.

For the record, I don't recommend sleeping in a fire station unless you're really used to it.

I was exhausted and incredibly sore when I arrived in Greenfield, but I was also energized by my completely unexpected success and warm greeting upon arrival.

In Greenfield, I met with more local press, the mayor and a few people who recognized me from my media onslaught from earlier in the day.

I still wasn't convinced I could really succeed. I still wasn't convinced kindness would be the rule of the day, but I found myself incredibly inspired at the day one and ready to see where this journey was going to take me.

It took me all over the place.

It took me to Shelbyville, Greensburg, North Vernon, Seymour, Scottsburg, Salem, Paoli, French Lick, Jasper, Huntingburg,

Evansville, Princeton, Vincennes, Sullivan, Linton, Bloomington, Spencer, Terre Haute, Clinton, Rockville, Crawfordsville, West Lafayette, Delphi, Logansport, Rochester, Plymouth, South Bend, Mishawaka, Elkhart, Goshen, Warsaw, Columbia City, Fort Wayne, Huntington, Wabash, Marion, Alexandria, Anderson, Noblesville, Carmel and back to Indianapolis.

I finished. I finished on time.

By the time I finished, I had traveled for 41 days and 1,086 miles alone by wheelchair across the state of Indiana. I'd traveled in virtually every type of weather imaginable ranging from hot, sunny days to thunderstorms to, yes, even a freak snowstorm down in Evansville.

There was this terrific photograph in the Evansville Courier-Press of me wheeling down U.S. 41 on my way into Evansville in a blinding snowstorm. I was completely nuts, but it was glorious. It sealed my reputation as a committed activist. My mantra became "Abuse doesn't end in the rain, snow, heat or storms. Our efforts to end it can't end either." I became obsessed with the idea that abuse survivors needed to know that there was someone out there willing to endure anything to make a difference.

I received the first of what would prove to be many awards in Shelbyville, Indiana while getting my first opportunity to speak in Greensburg, Indiana to a child abuse prevention council. While I'd always been comfortable with public speaking, my early attempts at speaking my truth were so laughably melodramatic that I look back now and cringe.

But, I was learning. I was gaining confidence in my voice and I was learning what I wanted and needed to say.

I was learning that I had a message and, perhaps even more surprisingly, I was learning that there were a lot of people who wanted to hear it. The invitations started pouring in on the road and word was traveling statewide that I was on the road.

I preached at a church in Salem, Indiana.

I struggled through the winding curves of Paoli and French Lick, Indiana. I was briefly arrested in Sullivan, Indiana by a sheriff who was convinced this dirty and exhausted guy on the side of the road was a vagrant. When he called his buddies in Vincennes, the city prior to Sullivan, I was promptly let go and helped along the way.

In Rockville, Indiana a dear Pentecostal preacher invited me to speak in his church (If he only knew!). With compassion and honesty, he pulled me aside at one point and said "You know. People would receive your message much better if you'd take better care of yourself." I've never forgotten his words.

I had my first physical breakdown on Mile-Long Hill in Delphi, Indiana and ended up transported to the local hospital by ambulance. Everyone in the ER recognized me and I was never charged a dime for the ambulance ride or hospital visit. Because of the physical breakdown, I'd lost some of my required medical supplies down a hill. A medical supply company owner from Terre Haute drove all the way in at 3am with fresh supplies.

Again, he never charged me a dime.

I made the mistake of arriving in South Bend on a Notre Dame football game day. So, um, the mayor was busy. Instead, I spent the night at the Wooden Nickel Inn talking to a small group of prostitutes about healing from sexual abuse.

They were among the best conversations I've ever had on the Tenderness Tour.

I broke down again in Columbia City, and this time actually had to take a day off. I was totally and completely exhausted emotionally and physically.

Every city. Every town. Every day. Every moment of every day. Miracle after miracle after miracle.

I could be in the middle of nothing but farmland, and someone would show up with water, food, a hug, a word of encouragement, a tip on people I could meet in the next town, a place to stay or a donation. It was constant and it never failed.

I can't lie. It was a lot of fun receiving awards and certificates and keys to cities, but what amazed me as I returned home was how I'd traveled alone along the roads of Indiana for 41 days and had never felt alone.

Complete and total strangers welcomed me into their homes, fed me, occasionally physically assisted me, nurtured me, guided me, advised me, supported me, encouraged me, affirmed me and showed me that I was wrong.

There is tenderness in the world.

I'd thought that I might return home free to just go ahead and kill myself, but quite the opposite happened. I came home realizing that all the old tapes that were playing in my head were wrong. I came home realizing that there was more than just a reason to live, I had a purpose in my life. It was going to be my life's mission to reach the unreachable, touch the untouchable and to find a way to love those who believe themselves to be unlovable. I came home realizing that if I wanted to live with the feelings I'd experienced on the Tenderness Tour, that I would have to make some really serious changes in my life.

A Reflection on Victoria

There are events, times and people in my life who helped steer me the right direction, then there are those cornerstones in my life.

Victoria is a cornerstone.

I remember being awed when my friend Valerie and her husband Steve asked me to be a godparent for Victoria.

I was amazed. Me? Have you actually met me? Have you seen how I live my life? Have you seen my home? Have you seen how I take care of myself? Have you sniffed around me lately? Me?

They trusted me with their child, and the first time I held Victoria as an infant my life was forever changed.

I didn't even hold children. Innocence scared me. I was afraid I would break them or hurt them or something along those lines. I was so nervous the first time I held her. I was afraid I'd drop her, move her the wrong way, hold her too tightly or hold her too loosely.

My heart was racing.

But, there she was. She was in my arms and she was perfect and peaceful and just the most delightful little human being ever.

She didn't seem hurt. She wasn't crying. She didn't seem to hate me.

I was madly in love with her. She was incredible. She was perfect in just about every way.

The Tenderness Tour had planted the seeds of change in my life, but Victoria brought the seeds to bloom. She made me want to be a better human being. I wanted to be a positive role model for her. I wanted to be a healthy adult in her life, even though I knew she was surrounded by healthy adults who loved her and who would raise her well. I didn't think she would ever actually "need" me, but there was no way I was going to be some absent, half-assed godparent. I wanted her to never have to question that she was loved.

I didn't want her to see me or hear about me abusing myself, being suicidal, drinking too much or otherwise acting stupid. It's not that I stopped being human, but I stopped allowing myself to resort to negative or self-destructive coping skills.

Victoria is a young adult now. She studies Criminal Justice at a Midwestern university and is just as delightful now as she was as a young child. She's gifted, intelligent, talented, compassionate and beautiful in every sense of the word.

I didn't really have anything to do with any of the above, but I do know that I've loved her every moment of every day since the day she was born.

I can only hope that I've improved her life in some small way, because she's truly brought me nothing but joy.

Discovering the Tenderness

The first few months following the first Tenderness Tour were traumatic. After all, my entire perspective on life was changing. I was no longer drowning in a sea of doubt, insecurity and fear. I experienced one brief period of self-destructive behavior, but for the most part I'd returned home with such a clear sense of purpose for my life that, quite literally, everything in my life began to change.

I returned home to Indianapolis after 41 days on the road with new connections, renewed connections and with the strength needed to let go of unhealthy, abusive connections. Rather than bouncing in and out of homelessness, I applied for and received Section 8 housing that allowed me to move into a clean, decent apartment in a safe neighborhood. It wasn't a perfect apartment, but it was the most stable that I had been in years and was where I would live for the next 6-7 years while taking other steps to get my life together.

Having gone on Social Security Disability following the failure of my first job and my first attempt in the world of academia, I decided that I was capable of achieving greater things. So, in addition to finding a stable home I found myself applying for and returning back to college for a second attempt at creating a better life for myself.

I applied at Martin University, a private college on Indy's eastside that specializes in the adult learner. I've always considered the school a "second chance" school, a school that emphasizes reaching out to the non-traditional learner. Martin University is a predominantly African-American university, a community in which I have always found much acceptance and safety.

By the end of my first semester at Martin University, I had discovered yet another valuable truth about myself.

I'm smart. Who knew? I spent my entire first semester under the guidance of Sister Marian Ruth, a Catholic nun who found herself winding down her academic career as a professor at this small college that existed in two older, inner-city buildings in a lower-income neighborhood. The professors at Martin University were often quite brilliant, but they were also typically more concerned with improving people's lives and changing the world than they were with gaining stature in the academic or professional world.

Sister Marian Ruth figured out very early on in the semester that I was an experiential learner. She could give me a written test that would serve up disappointing results indicating I just wasn't learning, but if she allowed me to find ways to create answers then the results were entirely different.

By the end of that first semester, I had earned my first ever semester of straight A's.

I admittedly thought this might be a fluke, the glorious result of my newfound inspiration and a professor with whom I had really connected.

But, it happened again the next semester. And again. And again.

In case you're wondering, I didn't have Sister Marian Ruth for every class. No, the truth was simple. I had a brain and was figuring out how to use it.

I graduated from Martin University in 1994 with a B.S. in Counseling Psychology and a Drama minor. I had a 4.0 GPA, graduated Summa Cum Laude and was ranked at the top of my class and served as a graduation speaker.

I blew everyone away at graduation by accomplishing a long-standing goal of walking down the aisle for graduation. I'd saved up and bought prosthetics myself because I so badly wanted the experience of walking down the aisle. While walking was not to be a long-term accomplishment, being able to do so on graduation day is still one of the highlights of my life.

Richard Propes

A Reflection on Father Hardin

The word majestic is what comes to mind when I contemplate Father Boniface Hardin, an extraordinary man who founded Martin University and who served as its spiritual guide even long after his retirement until his death early in 2012.

Father Hardin carried within himself the essence of Martin University, an essence defined by compassion for others, a dedication to improving lives, a belief in equal rights for all and a willingness to shake things up to accomplish all of the above.

I loved him more than the written word can possibly say.

While Martin has been somewhat updated in recent years, when I attended the school in the early 90's, most of the classrooms were in this old elementary school on three floors with no elevator. They had a mobility lift installed towards the end of my academic career, but for the majority of my years from 1991-1994 you could find me sitting on my butt and carrying my wheelchair up and down the flights of stairs to my classes.

I loved it. I wouldn't have changed it for anything. It felt symbolic of the fact that I was humbly crawling towards a better place in life. I was so incredibly grateful for the opportunity.

Father Hardin seemed to take a liking to me right away, though if I'm being honest I think he loved everyone. He had a flowing white beard with completely out of control white hair that made him resemble Frederick Douglass, a resemblance he capitalized on by frequently appearing as the great orator.

Father Hardin didn't just stimulate your intellect, he loved you in the quietest of ways. I still remember a time from a few years back when I'd been laid off from my job for several months. Times were rough and I was really close to losing everything despite trying really hard to find work. Father Hardin was one of my references, so I stayed in touch with him regularly. He asked me if I'd be willing to come speak to a staff meeting about my Tenderness Tour and life journey, an opportunity for which, of course, I said

"Yes!" immediately. I loved any opportunity to support Martin University, but I had no idea he'd set it all up to support me.

At the end of my presentation, I stayed over to speak with several professors and suddenly found in my hands an envelope with a substantial financial gift. He replied "You shared your gifts with us. We want to share our gifts with you."

This was the rule, not the exception with Father Hardin. It wasn't about money, but about the fact that this man could read your heart, mind and body language and figure out how to support you to your fullest potential. As my healing process in the 90's was really taking flight, Father Hardin became one of my first and greatest male role models.

Richard Propes

Winona Memorial Hospital

During my senior year at Martin University, I served as an intern at Winona Memorial Hospital. Winona was a small, for-profit hospital founded by Dr. Joseph Walther and named after his mother. It was a sort of healthcare outcast in Indianapolis, a lone wolf in a market filled with larger medical centers. I found myself placed on the Behavioral Health Unit, the placement that would eventually lead me to end my relationship with my therapist and the placement that would reveal that all those years of living in crisis had given me an almost uncanny ability to support others in crisis.

My placement at Winona was so successful that the day after my college graduation, I had a job offer in hand. I was later told by the director of the unit that one of the deciding factors was that I'd somehow gotten into the unit for my scheduled shift on a morning when we had eight fresh inches of snow on the ground. I was the only intern who made it in that day.

I think everyone in my life was a little stunned, not because I was working but because I was working in a field that could potentially trigger bad memories or a self-destructive relapse. Instead, I was learning how to take all of my life experiences and turn them into something good. It wasn't good that these things happened, but good was starting to come from these life experiences.

First, I was a milieu clinician or what amounted to a mental health technician with a degree. It was a rather basic position, but I loved it. I loved working!

It's not that I suddenly became an awesome professional. That's for sure! I was acknowledged as really good at my job, but I struggled mightily with self-care and personal appearance. Up until the day I went to work, I'd been supported with three days a week of home health care to assist with housecleaning and ADL's. Suddenly, I had to do everything myself. I was exhausted and not particularly good at things. Medical/personal things related to spina bifida, like bladder/bowel care, were and still are incredibly difficult to manage on my own and frequently things didn't go well.

My performance evaluations were almost funny in the way they would read "Richard does an incredible job, but needs to work on his personal hygiene." I hate the word hygiene.

For my first seven years at Winona, personal hygiene appeared on all my performance evaluations. I just couldn't figure things out. I even went to a counselor to learn how to do laundry more effectively. I tried hiring help, but that became too expensive.

Prior to one promotion, one supervisor even offered to throw in dry cleaning as a job perk. The really weird thing was that I started getting promoted anyway. I went from Milieu Clinician to Assessment Team, a position that put me on the frontlines doing crisis intervention in the emergency room setting.

I was in heaven. I was now doing work directly related to everything that I had ever experienced in my life. I have so many completely wonderful memories of completely unorthodox interventions that were successful. Of course, there were many sad stories along the way. But, I felt like I was making a difference in people's lives and I loved every moment of it.

Winona was a family. It was an amazing facility, even towards the end of its existence when a corporate takeover went awry. We never stopped caring about one another, and we had a reputation on the Behavioral Health Unit for being really good at what we did. I would eventually receive one more promotion, a move up to Admission Coordinator of the Behavioral Health Unit. It was in this position that I was named the hospital's "Employee of the Year" just a little over a year before the hospital closed.

It was during my time at Winona that I would finally find a church that felt like home, becoming ordained by The Church Within in Indianapolis after over two years of intensive study under their founding pastor, Rev. Louise Dunn. This allowed me to serve on the chaplaincy staff at Winona, as well, and I had the remarkable privilege of performing weddings, baptisms, funerals and other sacraments at Winona for both staff and patients.

Winona Memorial Hospital was torn down recently, the victim of a challenging healthcare market in Indianapolis and a final corporate ownership that sucked its finances dry supporting its other pet projects. It was sad to drive by the place that had fostered in me so much growth and to watch it being turned to dust.

The Tenderness Tour Journey

Even though I was becoming less and less of a "tender mess," The Tenderness Tour journey became deeply ingrained in my healing identity. For a solid year after my first Tenderness Tour, I found myself hitting the road on weekends visiting communities and appearing at smaller events. While I didn't do another long-distance Tenderness Tour at the time, I was doing smaller memorial walks and vigils along with numerous personal appearances. I was becoming comfortable with my voice, and I was learning how to use my voice in a way that respected my healing and was less traumatizing than my early appearances that too often sold the drama.

After spending most of 1989-90 following up on my first Tenderness Tour, I hit the road again in 1991 with a wheelchair tour from Indianapolis to Chicago. This was followed by a 1992 trip from Indianapolis to Cincinnati and a 1993 trip from Indianapolis to Lexington. I was becoming well known throughout the region as an activist for kids, but maybe even more for my honest, passionate and heartfelt presentations.

It was after the Lexington trip that the accolades and honors really started coming in, with my being commissioned a Kentucky Colonel by former Kentucky Governor Brereton Jones and a Sagamore of the Wabash in Indiana by former Indiana Governor Frank O'Bannon.

After a couple smaller Tenderness Tour events in 1994 and 1995, mostly because I had finally graduated from college and was now working full-time, I achieved a new high in 1996 when I traveled back to Chicago but, for the very first time, had a support team with me in the form of three nurses from Winona Hospital.

Having a support team was an incredibly new challenge, because it required me to both acknowledge I had needs and to allow someone to support those needs.

I wasn't very good at it, to be perfectly honest, and by the end of that 1996 trip my friendship with one of the nurses was so strained we were barely speaking to one another.

Since that first Tenderness Tour in 1989, I've traveled over 3,000 miles by wheelchair and Tenderness Tour events have raised close to $400,000 for children's organizations around the world. I've offered events all over the country, while speaking to groups ranging from a few people to a few thousand people.

I've offered at least one Tenderness Tour event every year since 1989, and in 2014 will celebrate my 25th anniversary with a special event I'm calling the "miracle mile," event. My plan is, for only the second time in the last twenty-five years of my life, to walk once again – one mile to symbolize the power of one person to make a difference in the world.

There have been literally dozens of other Tenderness Tour events where wheeling wasn't involved ranging from organized concerts to workshops to my absolute favorite, "Give a Girl a Chance," a CD compilation I produced in 2009 to celebrate the tour's 20th anniversary.

In addition to having wheeled over 3,000 miles and helped to raise nearly $400,000, the Tenderness Tour is the only all volunteer effort to have donated funds in every nation of the world. That was accomplished during another goofy idea of mine, "Tenderness Around the World," that happened during the 15th anniversary celebration.

A History of Tenderness

1989 Tenderness Tour

October 8, 1989:	Indianapolis to Greenfield
October 9, 1989:	Greenfield to Shelbyville
October 10, 1989:	Shelbyville to Greensburg
October 11, 1989:	Greensburg to North Vernon
October 12, 1989:	North Vernon to Seymour
October 13, 1989:	Seymour to Scottsburg
October 14, 1989:	Scottsburg to Salem
October 15, 1989:	Salem to Paoli
October 16, 1989:	Paoli to French Lick
October 17, 1989:	French Lick to Jasper
October 18, 1989:	Jasper to Huntingburg
October 19, 1989:	Huntingburg to Evansville
October 20, 1989:	Evansville to Princeton
October 21, 1989:	Princeton to Vincennes
October 22, 1989:	Vincennes to Sullivan
October 23, 1989:	Sullivan to Linton
October 24, 1989:	Linton to Bloomington
October 25, 1989:	Bloomington to Spencer
October 26, 1989:	Spencer to Terre Haute
October 27, 1989:	Terre Haute to Clinton
October 28, 1989:	Clinton to Rockville
October 29, 1989:	Rockville to Crawfordsville
October 30, 1989:	Crawfordsville to West Lafayette
October 31, 1989:	West Lafayette to Delphi
November 1, 1989:	Delphi to Logansport
November 2, 1989:	Logansport to Rochester
November 3, 1989:	Rochester to Plymouth
November 4, 1989:	Plymouth to South Bend
November 5, 1989:	South Bend to Mishawaka
November 6, 1989:	Mishawaka to Elkhart
November 7, 1989:	Elkhart to Goshen

November 8, 1989: Goshen to Warsaw
November 9, 1989: Warsaw to Columbia City
November 10, 1989: Columbia City to Fort Wayne
November 11, 1989: Fort Wayne to Huntington
November 12, 1989: Huntington to Wabash
November 13, 1989: Wabash to Marion
November 14, 1989: Marion to Alexandria
November 15, 1989: Alexandria to Anderson
November 16, 1989: Anderson to Noblesville
November 17, 1989: Noblesville to Carmel
November 18, 1989: Carmel to Back Home in Indy!

1990 Tenderness Tour
Small events were held in various cities visited on the 1989 tour. I stayed busy throughout the year.

1991 Tenderness Tour
June 19, 1991: Indianapolis to Lebanon
June 20, 1991: Lebanon to Frankfort
June 21, 1991: Frankfort to Flora
June 22, 1991: Flora to Monticello
June 23, 1991: Monticello to Francesville
June 24, 1991: Francesville to Lacrosse
June 25, 1991: Lacrosse to Crown Point
June 26, 1991: Crown Point to Gary
June 27, 1991: Gary to East Chicago
June 28, 1991: East Chicago to Chicago, IL

1992 Tenderness Tour
July 13, 1992: Indianapolis to Greenfield
July 14, 1992: Greenfield to Rushville
July 15, 1992: Rushville to Greensburg
July 16, 1992: Greensburg to Versailles
July 17, 1992: Versailles to Lawrenceburg

July 18, 1992: Lawrenceburg to Cincinnati, OH
July 19, 1992: Celebration back in Indy

1993 Tenderness Tour
August 8, 1993:   Indianapolis to Greenwood
August 9, 1993:   Greenwood to Franklin
August 10, 1993: Franklin to Columbus
August 11, 1993: Columbus to Seymour
August 12, 1993: Seymour to Salem
August 13, 1993: Salem to New Albany
August 14, 1993: New Albany to Louisville, KY
August 15, 1993: Louisville to Shelbyville, KY
August 16, 1993: Shelbyville to Frankfort, KY
August 17, 1993: Frankfort to Georgetown, KY
August 18, 1993: Georgetown to Lexington, KY
August 19, 1993: Day spent in Lexington, KY

1994 Tenderness Tour
November 19, 1994: Indianapolis, IN (56-mile, 1 day event)

1995 Tenderness Tour
April 1995: Indianapolis, IN event for children w/HIV

1996 Tenderness Tour
June 23, 1996: Indianapolis to Lebanon, IN
June 24, 1996: Lebanon to Frankfort
June 25, 1996: Frankfort to Lafayette
June 26, 1996: Lafayette to Reynolds/Monticello
June 27, 1996: Monticello to Rensselaer
June 28, 1996: Rensselaer to Demotte
June 29, 1996: Demotte to Crown Point
June 30, 1996: Crown Point to Gary
July 1, 1996:   Gary to East Chicago
July 2, 1996:   East Chicago to Chicago
July 3-4, 1996: Stay in Chicago for Events

1997 Tenderness Tour
October 3, 1997: Indianapolis to Greenwood
October 4, 1997: Greenwood to Mooresville
October 5, 1997: Mooresville to Plainfield
October 6, 1997: Plainfield to Brownsburg
October 7, 1997: Brownsburg to Zionsville
October 8, 1997: Zionsville to Carmel
October 9, 1997: Carmel to Lawrence
October 10, 1997: Lawrence to Indianapolis

1998 Tenderness Tour
April 30, 1998: Indianapolis to Greenwood
May 1, 1998:   Greenwood to Franklin
May 2, 1998:   Franklin to Columbus
May 3, 1998:   Columbus to Seymour
May 4, 1998:   Seymour to Scottsburg
May 5, 1998:   Scottsburg to Charlestown
May 6, 1998:   Charlestown to Jeffersonville
May 7, 1998:   Jeffersonville to New Albany
May 8, 1998:   Celebration in Indy

1999 Tenderness Tour
September 22-23, 1999: Indianapolis to Carmel
September 24-25, 1999: Carmel to Lebanon
September 26-27, 1999: Lebanon to Greencastle
September 28-29, 1999: Greencastle to Danville
September 30-Oct. 1, 1999: Danville to Indianapolis

2000 Tenderness Tour
September 26, 2000: Shelbyville, IN & Connersville, IN
September 27, 2000: Franklin, IN & Martinsville, IN
September 28, 2000: Bloomington, IN & Bedford, IN
September 29, 2000: Jasper, IN & Santa Claus, IN
September 30, 2000: Princeton, IN & Evansville, IN
October 1, 2000:   Day Off

October 2, 2000:   East Chicago, IN
October 3, 2000:   Valparaiso, IN & LaPorte, IN
October 4, 2000:   Elkhart, IN & Kendallville, IN
October 5, 2000:   Garrett, IN & Fort Wayne, IN
October 6, 2000:   Marion, IN & Anderson, IN
October 7-8, 2000:   Indianapolis, IN

2001 Tenderness Tour

April 16, 2001:   Warsaw, IN
April 17, 2001:   Indianapolis, IN
April 18, 2001:   Columbus, IN
April 19, 2001:   Day off
April 20, 2001:   Connersville, IN
August 5, 2001:   Indianapolis, IN
August 6, 2001:   Muncie, IN & Richmond, IN
August 7, 2001:   Shelbyville, IN & Franklin, IN
August 8, 2001:   Martinsville, IN & Bloomington, IN
August 9, 2001:   Seymour, IN & North Vernon, IN
August 10, 2001:   New Albany, IN
August 11, 2001:   Evansville, IN & Princeton, IN
August 12, 2001:   Terre Haute, IN & Lafayette, IN
August 13, 2001:   East Chicago, IN
August 14, 2001:   Valparaiso, IN & Knox, IN
August 15, 2001:   Elkhart, IN & Garrett, IN
August 16, 2001:   Fort Wayne, IN & Huntington, IN
August 17, 2001:   Kokomo, IN
August 18, 2001:   Indianapolis, IN
September 29, 2001: Carmel, IN

2002 Tenderness Tour

April 20-21, 2002:   Kendallville & LaGrange, IN
April 23, 2002:   Indianapolis, IN
April 28, 2002:   Indianapolis, IN
April 29, 2002:   Frankfort, IN

May 24, 2002: New Albany, IN
October 26, 2002: Indianapolis, IN

2003 Tenderness Tour
March 20, 2003: Martinsville, IN
September 6, 2003: Indianapolis, IN (25-mile ICADV Event)
September 25, 2003: Chesterfield, IN

2004 Tenderness Tour
April 25, 2004: 1-mile events in six Indiana cities.
May 17, 2004: St. Louis, MO
May 18, 2004: Orlando, FL
May 26, 2004: Glendale, AZ
May 27, 2004: Phoenix, Tempe, Scottsdale & Mesa, AZ
May 30, 2004: Denver, CO
October 1, 2004: ICADV Event in Indy

2005 Tenderness Tour
July 2, 2005: Peoria, IL
September 10, 2005: ICADV Event in Indy
November 5, 2005: Duluth, MN

2006 Tenderness Tour
April 23, 2006: Broad Ripple, IN
August 16, 2006: Richmond, IN
September 23, 2006: ICADV Event

2007 Tenderness Tour
February 11, 2007: Goshen, IN
April 1, 2007: Indianapolis & Lawrence, IN
April 25, 2007: IUPUI Take Back The Night
April 26, 2007: ICADV Event in Indy

2008 Tenderness Tour
January 1, 2008: Indianapolis, IN (31-mile Event)

April 16, 2008:	IUPUI Take Back The Night
August 16, 2008:	ICADV Event in Indy

2009 Tenderness Tour

June 28, 2009:	San Diego, CA
August 15, 2009:	ICADV Event in Indy
October 7, 2009:	Terre Haute, IN
October 8, 2009:	Terre Haute to Brazil
October 9, 2009:	Brazil to Greencastle
October 10, 2009:	Greencastle to Danville
October 11, 2009:	Danville to Indianapolis
October 12, 2009:	Indianapolis to Greenfield
October 13, 2009:	Greenfield to Knightstown
October 14, 2009:	Knightstown to Cambridge City
October 15, 2009:	Cambridge City to Richmond

2010 Tenderness Tour

July 5, 2010:	Pittsburgh, PA
August 14, 2010:	ICADV Event in Indy

2011 Tenderness Tour

August 2011:	ICADV Event in Indy

And the journey continues!

11 Lessons From A Life On the Road

1. We all can get along. Really. The vast majority of us have the same wants, needs and desires in life. We may have different paths for getting there, but the vision is the same. It is possible to get along with everyone if we drop the bullshit labels that only serve to separate us. Let's love one another. I'm not simplifying anything. It really is that simple.

2. Happiness is not a goal. Happiness is a choice. You can choose it right now, regardless of your circumstances. You can choose happiness, then you can go about creating life circumstances that help you maintain it. But, if you think the stuff will get you to happiness you're always going to find yourself falling short.

3. Diversity is to be embraced. Why? Because we're not all that different anyway. Black? White? Hispanic? Asian? Who cares? Conservative? Liberal? Progressive? Who cares? Gay? Straight? I've learned time and time again that people I'd pigeon-holed into a certain corner were far more awesome than I'd ever expected.

4. We need each other. Sometimes the needs are physical, sometimes they are emotional. The point is that we're brought into this life dependent and we're meant to live it out together. This doesn't mean that we'll all get married and have a family, but I believe we're all meant to live in community with one another.

5. Be yourself. Just you as you are. Sure, you can work on improving yourself. That's great. But, life is too short to get hung up on being cool or having all the best stuff. Be vulnerable enough to show up in your strengths and weaknesses.

6. Listen. Listen to your friends. Listen to God, however, you experience God. Listen to nature. Listen to your gut. Slow down the distractions and listen.

7. Give. Give of yourself. Give of your stuff. Don't have much? Give anyway. Receiving is overrated. Giving is underrated. Life always gets better when you're serving others.

8. Make mistakes. Make lots and lots of mistakes. You'll be way ahead of those people afraid to try and along the way you'll pick up a ton of successes.

9. Anger is okay. Abuse, violence or cruelty are never okay.

10. Touch can be a loving experience.

11. Every single moment of your life is another opportunity to give and receive love. Use your moments wisely.

Richard Propes

A Reflection on Victor

My defining moment with Victor came a few years back while we were out for one of our usual drives. These drives were therapeutic for Victor and I, because they afforded us the opportunity to just relax and have low pressure, honest conversations at a casual pace. I loved these drives and the conversations that often resulted from them.

At this time in my life, I was still pretty deeply bound in shame over my body and how it functioned. While Victor obviously knew I was disabled, I'd never really discussed the intimate details of my disability and the ways in which it often did impact my life.

On this particular night, Victor and I had been out for quite some time when I felt the "urge" to go to the bathroom. I was prone to bladder spasms, and admitting this was just too far out of my comfort zone. Well, my silence didn't make the problem go away and before long I'd had, well, an accident.

Humiliation!

I think he could tell I was uncomfortable, but he didn't quite grasp right away what was going on. Finally, as we neared our destination, I had no choice but to tell him the truth.

"Um, Victor. I've pissed in your car."

In this moment, Victor was simply extraordinary. He, in fact, said very little because very little could have been said. He dropped me off and dealt with the car. When the time was right, we had a wonderfully honest and loving conversation.

I have never bonded well with men, but Victor and I clicked almost right away when we first met during my first college stint at Indiana University-Purdue University at Indianapolis. We were active in the Theater Department, and our friendship blossomed.

In right about 25 years of friendship, Victor and I have never actually argued. Sure, we've occasionally had to address hurt feelings or miscommunication. However, it's always been done quickly so an open wound wouldn't become infected.

Victor was the one who said the psychiatrist was nuts for putting me in the hospital on Christmas Eve one year after one of my suicidal gestures.

Victor has supported and/or been a part of virtually every fund-raiser, special event or crazy idea I've ever concocted. That's a lot of ideas.

In many ways, our personalities have borrowed from one another. I've become more assertive over the years, while he's become more warm and fuzzy.

When I think of the original male role model I had in the early days of my healing process, Victor is right at the top of my list.

He tried desperately to get me away from my wife Laura, and was more than a little irritated when I finally confessed (YEARS later!) that I'd actually married her.

He correctly predicted that my last relationship wouldn't last more than nine months, though we lasted a year just to piss him off.

My parents have sworn more than once that Victor and I are a couple, a fact that made me chuckle once he finally decided to "come out" with me (Duh! I already knew!).

Truthfully, I think we're more like brothers. There's never been a day he didn't improve my life simply by being present, and I can't imagine my life without him.

Richard Propes

A Reflection on Melissa's Suicide

I came home from one of my life highlights, sharing a devotion at Church of the Brethren's Annual Conference in Pittsburgh, to the news that one of my oldest and best friends had committed suicide.

I'm three lines into this reflection and I'm already crying.

Melissa and I met as theater students in college. She was slightly older than me, married and incredibly talented. She was the assistant director on the musical "Working," the show I was performing in when I accidentally placed one of my crutches off the side of the stage and danced right off of it. It was an injury that would eventually lead to amputation of both feet, mostly because I did a horrid job of self-care.

Melissa took remarkably good care of me as I became determined to finish the show, even with my right leg in a cast. I succeeded, at least partially because she refused to allow me to fail.

Melissa didn't know it at the time, but my wife had just committed suicide and I was frequently living on the street. She did know that I was in a downward spiral, and while we worked together on a variety of theatrical projects she became an endlessly nurturing presence as my emotions became more and more out of whack.

She would eventually take a gun out of my hands. It was loaded. I was ready and serious.

Melissa eventually left Indianapolis to attend graduate school at Vanderbilt University pursuing her dream career of helping at-risk children.

It wouldn't be until her return to Indy several years later that I would learn that we had similar backgrounds marred by severe abuse. By the time she returned, Melissa had her own struggles with mental health and suicide. Our reunion, however, seemed to do wonders for both of us even though I'd already started living in a much better place.

Melissa had always been quite comfortable with my disability and my emotional struggles. While I'd not revealed the intimate details of my life with disability to her, Melissa and I shared a remarkable vulnerability with one another and this only grew once she returned.

Much like me, Melissa had spent a good portion of her healing journey reaching out to others. She worked with the disabled, worked with at-risk kids and had even served as foster parent for one profoundly disabled teenager. She was a remarkable human being, though she never really quite grasped that fact.

One night, Melissa and I were hanging out while her husband was at work and I'd had a bit too much wine to drink. After I panicked thinking I was coughing up blood (It was red wine, geez!), Melissa decided I was too impaired to drive home. She drove me home, helped me to bed and promptly learned lots of things about my disability that surprised her.

In some ways, I do believe this discovery hurt our friendship. In some ways, it made it stronger. She became one of my primary physical supports once she realized that my needs were far greater than she'd ever realized. I'd been struggling physically and her physical presence made a huge difference in my life's quality.

The day before I left for my church conference, Melissa and I met for coffee. I asked her to please not call frequently as I really needed to focus on my obligations, though I made it clear she could call in case of an emergency.

I remember saying to her "I can't always respond right away. I just can't. I have so much going on and I have my own body that's giving me fits. But, I love you. I always have. I always will. There's nothing you can do to make that go away."

Then, I came back from Pittsburgh and Melissa had gone away.

There aren't words, really, to describe how angry and hurt I still am by Melissa's suicide. She knew better. She knew that things get better. They always did and they always do.

She'd spent most of her adult life teaching children and adults that things could get better and that there is always hope. Her suicide completely invalidated all of that ... At least it did to me.

This thing, this impulse, this suicide has become her legacy. She was an amazing and intelligent woman who accomplished miracles with children whom many others could never reach. She had this amazing ability to reach someone and love someone and guide someone exactly where they were at and to guide them to a better place.

Why couldn't she ever do this for herself?

I spent a good month or so after Melissa's suicide e-mailing, texting, calling or seeing my friend Amy nearly every day. I'm grateful that Amy never missed a beat during this time, because virtually every day during this time I thought about joining Melissa.

I even went to Gander Mountain once to look at guns, but I decided they were too expensive.

One day, I even crawled up the flight of steps to her apartment just because I needed to be there. I gave serious thought to renting the place, though I finally convinced myself it would be really creepy to go into the rental office and demand that exact apartment.

I've always been one to respect someone's choices, but I have to be honest. I don't respect this one. This one was stupid. It was wrong. It was hurtful and selfish and now allows her daughter to grow up having to say "My mom killed herself." That really pisses me off.

Most of all, Melissa, I just really miss you.

Hallelujah Moments

Love is the key.

Every moment that we seek it.

Every moment that we find it.

Every moment that we grieve it.

Every moment that we learn what it is.

Every moment that we learn what it's not.

Every moment that we get destroyed, but decide to love again.

Every moment that we give it.

Every moment that we receive it.

Every moment that we teach it.

Every moment that we remember rightly.

Every moment that we remember wrongly, but decide to choose again.

Every moment that we surrender.

Every moment that we cower.

Every moment in our lives where love is all that matters.

Every moment that we fight like hell so that someone will never forget it.

That is love.

That is Hallelujah.

100 Hallelujahs

1. Barney Fife coming to the rescue of my parents so that I could be born.

2. I've seen a photo of my father holding me with a paper Santa Claus on the staircase. I had to be no more than two-years-old. I don't remember it, but it reminds me of the father/son relationship.

3. The doctors and nurses who saved my life when I was born, including Mrs. Stubbs, and who managed to do help bring to life a baby who has proven to be a miracle over and over again.

4. My first best friend, Heidi.

5. My first teacher, Mrs. Pruitt. You not only taught me well, but you recognized my giftedness and helped get me mainstreamed into public schools.

6. Mrs. Zimmer, my first teacher at Central Elementary School. You made third grade much less frightening.

7. Mrs. Dillon, my fourth-grade teacher who hated Jehovah's Witnesses and tried hard to fail me. Boy, you came close.

8. Mrs. Foster, my junior high guidance counselor. You thought it was a good idea to spend more time with Jeff. You were so completely clueless.

9. All my counselors at Camp Riley at Bradford Woods. You were the highlight of many summers. You rescued me from chaos and celebrated me.

10. My first public school friend, Ronnie Crist. You were the first one who wasn't scared of my disability and didn't tease me about it. I've never forgotten you.

11. Jehovah's Witnesses. You represent the best and worst of my childhood. You taught me the importance of friends and family, but you also taught me God is more than simply a theological statement.

12. Jeff. You tried to destroy my body and spirit, but couldn't. You taught me that love is more powerful than hate, peace more powerful than violence. You taught me to look in the mirror and see beauty and strength rather than scars, a curved spine, a body that doesn't always work and the damage you inflicted.

13. Valerie. You taught me that love isn't just about saying "I love you," but about showing up time and time again. It's about embracing someone so tightly that you don't give up on them even when everyone else does. It's about sitting with them, listening to them, challenging them, inspiring them and believing in them.

14. My father. Childhood was occasionally wonderful, frequently horrible. You were angry, bitter, insecure and self-centered. Then, you did the unthinkable and chose your wife and child over your insecurities, your alcohol and your past. You've never looked back and you've become someone who truly inspires me. You first said "I love you" when I was in my 30's. You meant it.

15. My mother. Webster has a picture of you next to the definition of loyalty. You steadfastly refuse to turn on your friends, your family and your children despite mistake after mistake, betrayal after betrayal. You taught me that love doesn't go away.

16. My brother. You and I managed to learn how to say "I Love you" and to hug despite not a lot of role models for it. We're incredibly different, but incredibly close because we

understand. On my list of favorite people in the world, you and Victoria are at the top.

17. Putt-Putt was the first thing I was really good at. I played on the junior national team. Yes, they really had one!

18. Mrs. Jefferson and Mrs. Booth, my high school speech coaches. You both believed in and supported this public speaker who never brought home a blue ribbon but who tried hard and showed up week after week. You challenged me, supported me, encouraged me and nurtured me without ever realizing what a huge difference you were making in my life.

19. I was on "The Brain Game" in high school, the first sign that perhaps there was more brain power going on than I'd previously thought.

20. Junior Achievement. You taught me that I could be a leader. I still think my win as "President of the Year" my senior year was one of the bigger upsets around. You instilled in me a work ethic, a drive and the belief that I could start a project and complete it to excellence.

21. Mrs. Albrecht. You were the high school nurse who seemed to deal most often with my ostomy.

22. Dr. Mitchell. You were the doctor who came up with a way to get rid of the ostomy. You cared as much about quality of life as you did about function of life.

23. All the healthcare professionals who have worked to make my life so extraordinary throughout 50+ surgeries and more than a few setbacks.

24. Dorothy and J. Edgar. You seemed limitless in your imagination and were the first ones who agreed to cast a

disabled actor in non-disabled roles. You accepted, guided, advised, supported and nurtured my talent. You cast me in the musical "Working" as a dancing tie salesman. I was a paraplegic on crutches.

25. Victor. You have been a friend since before I knew how to be one. You've traveled alongside me through life's many peaks and valleys, joys and sorrows.

26. Melissa. My first memory of love is you sitting backstage with me during the musical "Working." I'd fallen off the stage a week earlier, but was determined to complete the show even with my foot in a cast. You were by my side the entire time. We had a common ground in our severely traumatic backgrounds, but we spent our entire lives proving you could overcome it until you took your own life. I still miss you.

27. Lisa. You received the gift of my "voluntary virginity." You were the perfect "first time." You were loving, gentle, passionate, funny and accepting. I've still got the Jan Saudek print you gave me as my first Christmas present on the wall, "Theater of Life."

28. Winning the collegiate forensics state championship my freshman year at IUPUI in Original Oratory.

29. Playing the social worker in "Whose Life Is It Anyway?" at IUPUI.

30. Playing the judge in "Whose Life Is It Anyway?" at Christian Theological Seminary.

31. Getting kicked out of the Vineyard Christian Fellowship in Indianapolis. It illustrated for me the pastor I never wanted to be.

32. Joanna. You taught me how to kiss. You taught well.

33. Getting married. It was ill-advised, but it started off with two people fighting like hell to overcome their past. You taught me to never let go, always show "I love you" and to cherish every moment that I get with those I love.

34. Getting engaged two additional times to Christina and Melissa, respectively.

35. The Therapist. You risked everything to show me that there is always hope. You taught me that touch can be a loving experience.

36. Father Hardin and everyone at Martin University. Attending Martin University was 3+ years of hallelujah moments. I discovered my intelligence, my heart, my path and my faith during my time at Martin.

37. Robyn, Fran, Debbie, Melissa, Amy, Michelle, Nadine and anyone else who has ever reached through my fear and shame to help me out with my ADL's.

38. The guy who disguised himself as a woman so I'd fly out to San Francisco to meet him. You taught me that I'm willing to go to great lengths for love, but you also taught me that I refuse to be lied to in the process.

39. Prevent Child Abuse Indiana. You supported my first several years of healing. You encouraged, nurtured, supported and celebrated with me. Most of all, you "believed."

40. Harriet Clare. You owned the bookstore that first carried my original poetry collection, "Imaginary Crimes." You've supported and celebrated me for many years now.

41. The Tenderness Tour has provided hundreds of hallelujah moments all on its own. From middle of the night ER visits to volunteers who travel hundreds of miles to participate, the Tenderness Tour has provided the key vehicle through which I've learned to love, laugh, be tender and be present.

42. In 2009, I produced my first benefit CD. "Give a Girl a Chance" included 19 artists celebrating 20 years of the Tenderness Tour. It reminded me of just how true it is that I'm willing to do just about anything to accomplish my goals.

43. Victoria. You are love personified.

44. Becoming an uncle to three delightful, sensitive, intelligent and spirited boys.

45. My Aunt Nancy. The hardest thing I've ever done as a minister was the funeral for your son, Billy. Of anyone in my family, you were always the most comfortable with my disability. You didn't always know what you were doing, but you always did it with love and compassion and respect.

46. Sister Marian Ruth Johnson. You committed yourself to learning how I learn. You succeeded.

47. Breaking up with Melissa. I was far enough in my healing process that it really, really hurt. It also taught me that just because you love someone, it doesn't mean you should be together. Relationships require more. Besides, no one should ever get engaged with Madonna's "True Blue" in the background.

48. Appearing as Captain Freeheart at a benefit. I look sexy in tights. Admit it. You can picture it.

49. Linda. You were a student nurse during the reversal of my ostomy. You seemed dismayed when I remarked that I never wanted to marry because it would be asking someone to live with everything I have to live with. You thought I misunderstood what love was all about.

50. Buck. You were my first and only dog. You were a 14-year-old abused beagle. I thought we were perfect for each other, but I couldn't erase the memories of my childhood trauma. I finally sent you away, because I refused to hurt you.

51. Living in my car. Twice. It taught me the importance of having a home and being a home for one another.

52. The birth and death of Jennifer Lynn. Learning of your life reminded me that I can create beauty in the world, while your death inspires me to continue protecting children.

53. Becoming an ordained minister in The Church Within.

54. Becoming a licensed minister in Church of the Brethren, followed by my acceptance into Bethany Theological Seminary.

55. Graduating Summa Cum Laude from Martin University. I think every human being needs that one time in their lives when they achieve perfection. This was one of mine.

56. The evening I peed in Victor's car. It opened the door to the deepening of an already incredible friendship.

57. My sexual abuse. I'm not grateful for the abuse, but for the many ways in which I've learned how to live and love better because of it.

58. The day that my girlfriend at the time, Michelle, walked into my bedroom wearing nothing but a diaper. It was her way

of saying "I don't care how disabled you are. I don't care how your body functions." It's the single most romantic thing anyone has ever done for me.

59. Shopping for shoes. You haven't really lived until you've gone shoe shopping with a footless man. It's one of my favorite things to do, and I love that several of my friends have joined me for it.

60. Having both feet amputated. This is what triggered the memories of my abuse and forced me to deal with it. I had to deal with my body image issues and finally learn better self-care.

61. Attempting suicide. It taught me how to be there for others experiencing the same feelings. It also brought me to the point of being about as fearless as a human being can get.

62. My home break-in. Within hours, I had my door replaced and my home cleaned up by friends whom I've learned always seem to be by my side in good times and bad.

63. The poetry reading fund-raiser that served as my first outreach event. It only raised $10, but it convinced me that I could use my talent to make the world a better place.

64. The miscarriage my girlfriend experienced. For the second time, I lost a child. Years of grief all snowballed into this period of my life, while I finally was able to acknowledge my own regret over not being a husband or father.

65. Interviewing actress Tanna Frederick. I've interviewed quite a few people in the film industry, but Tanna and I had this marvelous 2+ hour conversation. It made me want to completely alter the way I do interviews and approach my work in film. It also really made me want to meet Tanna.

66. Winning the "Sagamore of the Wabash" Award, one of Indiana's highest awards for community service. Awards typically mean very little to me, but I'll admit being recognized for serving my home state was just amazing for me.

67. Publishing "Imaginary Crimes," my first poetry collection. It was graphic, violent and bordering on obscene. It was me reclaiming my voice and refusing to compromise the truth.

68. Becoming a member of the Indiana Film Journalists Association. I stumbled back into writing, something that brought me great joy for most of my life but then something that was put aside as my life took a different direction. To be recognized by my peers as a professional film critic is, as Ferris Bueller would say, "Choice."

69. The suicides of all those I know who have made that choice including Christina, Lisa, Melissa, Michael, Laura, Diana and others. You remind me to never stop trying to plant hope in the world and to never go a day without saying "I love you."

70. Rose, my director for the play "Whose Life Is It Anyway?" at CTS. You had the guts to say "You smell like death," a reminder that I had downward spiraled into a seriously self-destructive place.

71. The day that Melissa took the gun out of my hands.

72. The day that John Hiatt came on the radio right as I had a gun to my head and started singing "Have a Little Faith In Me."

73. The first time I held Victoria.

74. Being attacked in the tunnels underneath the campus of IUPUI while I was homeless. It forced me to re-evaluate this whole homeless thing, while also forcing me to deal with how my current choices were impacted by my traumatic memories.

75. Dating Kelly from Cape Cod. It's hard to have low self-esteem when a woman is flying halfway across the country to spend a weekend with you.

76. The first time I was asked to offer the prayer at my family's Thanksgiving gathering.

77. Looking for snakes with my cousins while visiting my grandparents' Kentucky farm. We found them, too!

78. The day that Paul and Sally came over to help move out one mattress and move in another. I'm always tremendously embarrassed when someone learns the intimate details of my disability. Paul, being Paul, simply responded "I'm amazed how well you do."

79. Preaching. It's my nirvana.

80. Having the chance to do work as a film critic on "Sandy on the Scene," an Indianapolis-based entertainment news show. It has taught me the ways in which I'm still insecure physically, while challenging me to deal with the memories of being photographed as a child.

81. Rev. Louise Dunn. She believed in my ministry and gave me opportunities to succeed and fail.

82. Getting my pants caught in my wheelchair while climbing out of my car. How many guys can claim picking up an exotic dancer because she helps you untangle the pants you lost while climbing into your wheelchair?

83. My goddaughter's high school graduation.

84. Speaking of my goddaughter, there's that time she and her mother showed up for the Tenderness Tour's 10th Anniversary celebration. It was completely unexpected.

85. Wheeling across Chicago's Lakeshore Drive after having just traveled from Indianapolis by wheelchair. It's likely the most beautiful scenery I've experienced on the Tenderness Tour.

86. Getting my "tender mess" tattoo.

87. Meeting writer/director Robert Zappia. He's written both "Halloween H20" and "Christmas Is Here Again," a reminder that we can put all of who we are into our creative endeavors.

88. Amy Beery. During the span of about 6 weeks, I experienced surgery, the suicide of my best friend and a home break-in. Amy was there for all of it. Amy is always there for all of it.

89. Christmas gifts from my brother. He always thinks they suck and, with the exception of that dreaded Axe aftershave, they almost always are completely awesome.

90. Leslie Fuller-Knox. You walked right into my last suicide attempt. Or was it my final suicide attempt? You had no clue, but you were absolutely perfect in every way.

91. Nissa. You've allowed me to use photos of your daughter on my benefit CD, and now you're allowing me to use a remarkable dance composition as part of this book's live readings. We've never even met, but our healing journeys seem to have become woven together. You also serve to remind me every day that a survivor can be a remarkable, loving parent.

92. Being called into ministry by Northview Church of the Brethren. It's amazing to me that this body of intelligent, compassionate and gifted human beings believes in my ministry.

93. Getting massages with Elizabeth Aldora. You took my physical insecurities and nurtured them. You treated my curved spine with a hole in it like it's sacred ground. Actually, I'm pretty sure it is sacred ground to you.

94. My 31-day hunger strike. It wasn't the best idea I've ever had, but it taught me about perseverance, self-care and vision.

95. Flying out of a Chicago gay bar completely wasted only to forget there was a step at the entrance. I went flying face forward out of my wheelchair, while my friend Victor doubled over laughing. A woman pulled over her vehicle and gave Victor the dirtiest look for laughing. Among a lifetime of funny moments, this one's a highlight for Victor and I.

96. Having sex. I almost remember it. What I remember is that it reminds me that Jeff didn't destroy me and that when someone really wants to be with you they will work with you to create a passionate, meaningful encounter.

97. Not having sex. Because of my background, I've always highly valued pure friendships. There's something special about realizing you can be loved and don't have to perform.

98. Posing naked for an art school. It made me realize that there is always someone, or many someones, who will find you beautiful.

99. Skydiving, Bungee Jumping and all my other extreme acts. Because they reinforce my commitment to learn how to live and love without fear.

100. Writing this book. I'm being honest, telling secrets, surrendering and trusting the process.

101. The list really does go on and on!

What are your hallelujah moments?

The Hallelujah Life

I have a ritual that I've performed every single day for nearly twenty years.

Every single day, I tell one person they are beautiful.

It can be a friend, a stranger, a co-worker, a peer or someone else. This person can be male or female, any age or any race or any size. I may not always use the word beautiful, but I never use the word sexy. The word sexy does not equal beautiful.

You're already living The Hallelujah Life.

You simply have to surrender to it.

The Hallelujah Life isn't pop theology or a supermarket self-help book.

The Hallelujah Life doesn't require reading a book, taking a class or achieving the thirteenth degree of enlightenment.

The Hallelujah Life is simple.

It's about love.

It's about surrendering yourself to the moments in our lives when we're forced to choose between love and hate or peace and conflict. Every moment when we choose love becomes our hallelujah moment.

Every moment when we rise up out of the ashes of defeat and choose to try again becomes a hallelujah moment.

Every moment when we have been hurt by love or something disguised as love but we choose to risk it all again becomes a hallelujah moment.

Every moment when we look in the mirror and see past our scars, curves, lines and hurts becomes a hallelujah moment.

Every moment when we offer an act of kindness for no reason at all becomes a hallelujah moment.

Every moment that we surrender to fully experiencing our joys and sorrows, victories and defeats becomes a hallelujah moment.

Every moment when we overcome our past, break our cycles, manage our addictions and confront our fears becomes a hallelujah moment.

Every moment when we offer one another vulnerability becomes a hallelujah moment.

Every moment that we dance with abandon, sing out of town, giggle uncontrollably and hug like we mean it becomes a hallelujah moment.

Every moment when we stop dissing our ability becomes a hallelujah moment.

Every hallelujah moment becomes, in turn, a hallelujah life.

ABOUT THE AUTHOR

Richard Propes is the founder and publisher for The Independent Critic, a communal film website combining film criticism, insightful and entertaining interviews and a strong devotion to peace, nonviolence & justice issues featuring "Reel Hope," an online database of celebrity philanthropy and community service. The Independent Critic is ranked in the Top 20 of all web-based film review websites. Propes is the author of "Imaginary Crimes" and "Secret Heart" along with four produced plays and also founded "The Gimp Goes Shopping," a customer service blog with a disability focus. A longtime freelance film critic for a variety of publications, Propes is the founder and Executive Director for the Tenderness Tour and has traveled over 3,000 miles raising nearly $500,000 for children's organizations worldwide since 1989. Propes serves as the Artistic Director for Indiana's first cause-oriented film festival, the Heart n' Sole Film Festival. Propes has won numerous awards for his child advocacy, most notably the highest awards for service in Indiana and Kentucky, "Sagamore of the Wabash" and "Order of Kentucky Colonels" along with the Donna J. Stone Award, Prevent Child Abuse America's highest award nationally for volunteer service in the area of child abuse prevention.

Richard's inspiring and often funny outlook on life has entertained, inspired and encouraged children, youth and adults. Richard's message of perseverance, faith in people and overcoming challenges is perfect for a variety of audiences and can be tailored to corporate, faith-based, academic and conference settings. For information on having Richard appear for your group, please contact:

Emerson Speakers Bureau
P.O. Box 241245
Indianapolis, IN 46224
Phone: 317-698-9652
Fax: 317-227-0522
www.emersonspeakersbureau.com

www.ingramcontent.com/pod-product-compliance
Lightning Source LLC
Chambersburg PA
CBHW060812050426
42449CB00008B/1643